The Mentor's Guidebook

The Mentor's Guidebook

Unleashing Your Potential to Inspire and Retain New Teachers

Vince Bustamante
Tim Cusack
Wayne Davies

Foreword by Franita Ware

CORWIN

For information:

Corwin
A Sage Company
2455 Teller Road
Thousand Oaks, California 91320
(800) 233-9936
www.corwin.com

Sage Publications Ltd.
1 Oliver's Yard
55 City Road
London EC1Y 1SP
United Kingdom

Sage Publications India Pvt. Ltd.
Unit No 323-333, Third Floor, F-Block
International Trade Tower Nehru Place
New Delhi 110 019
India

Sage Publications Asia-Pacific Pte. Ltd.
18 Cross Street #10-10/11/12
China Square Central
Singapore 048423

Vice President and Editorial Director: Monica Eckman
Senior Publisher: Jessica Allan
Senior Content Development Editor: Mia Rodriguez
Senior Editorial Assistant: Natalie Delpino
Production Editor: Vijayakumar
Copy Editor: Melinda Masson
Typesetter: TNQ Tech Pvt. Ltd.
Proofreader: Girish Sharma
Indexer: TNQ Tech Pvt. Ltd.
Cover Designer: Gail Buschman
Marketing Manager: Olivia Bartlett

Printed and bound by CPI Group (UK) Ltd, Croydon, CR0 4YY

ISBN 978-1-0719-6457-6

This book is printed on acid-free paper.

25 26 27 28 29 10 9 8 7 6 5 4 3 2 1

Contents

About the Authors

Vince Bustamante, EdD, is a Calgary-based author, instructional coach, curriculum content developer, and educational consultant. Vince specializes in working with teachers, leadership teams, schools, and school districts in implementing high-impact strategies and systems. With a strong background in implementation, assessment, and deep learning, he is passionate about understanding and evaluating teachers' impact. Having worked with schools and school districts across North America and internationally, he brings a wide variety of experience and perspectives when looking at school improvement, pedagogical and leadership development, and implementation of high-impact strategies across school environments. Vince's doctoral research focused on the sustainable implementation of professional learning across school districts, and the impact of long-term school partnerships.

Vince has coauthored two best-selling books with Corwin: *Great Teaching by Design* and *The Assessment Playbook for Distance and Blended Learning*. His other title, *Leader Ready: Four Pathways to Prepare Aspiring School Leaders*, is also available from Corwin. You can find more information about him at www.vincebustamante.com.

Timothy P. Cusack, EdD, has over 32 years of experience as a classroom teacher, assistant principal, principal, and superintendent. Having taught in rural boards in northern and southern Alberta, Tim also has 10 years of experience as a school leader (K–12) and eight years of experience as a system leader of a large urban board in Edmonton. Tim currently serves as the Dean of Education of Concordia University of Edmonton (CUE) where he leads a teacher preparation program (after degree in education) and a master of education in educational leadership program. His doctoral research focuses on new teacher preparation, teacher mentorship, and leadership development. His dissertation (University of Portland, 2020), which centered on preparing aspiring school leaders, evolved into his first book with Corwin: *Leader Ready: Four Pathways to Prepare Aspiring School Leaders* (2023).

Tim has worked with school jurisdictions across Canada and the United States in sharing his passion for leadership development and teacher mentorship. His service to public education has been recognized through the Council of School Leadership Distinguished Leadership Award (2014) and the Queen Elizabeth II Platinum Jubilee Medal (2023).

Tim also serves as a Naval Warfare Officer in the Royal Canadian Navy and brings a wealth of leadership experience having served now for over 35 years. In addition to his role of dean, Tim is currently the commanding officer of HMCS *Nonsuch*, Edmonton's naval reserve division. His experience in K–12 education, postsecondary leadership, and military leadership adds richness and depth to his work as an educational consultant and author.

More information about Tim may be found at www.timothycusack.com.

Wayne Davies, EdD, is the director of student teaching at the University of Winnipeg where he also teaches. Prior to this role, he spent 32 years as a teacher and school leader. He has taught and led in many settings including on the Lax Kw'alaams reserve in British Columbia, Canada, as well as in rural and urban school divisions in Manitoba. As a principal in Selkirk, Wayne was part of the nationally acclaimed BOSS Guitar Works project, which he eventually wrote about in his novel *The Guitar Principal*. In 2014, Wayne was recognized as one of Canada's top 40 school leaders and is a Distinguished Alumnus at the University of Manitoba for his community work. A citizen of the Red River Métis, Wayne holds an EdD in educational leadership from the University of Western Ontario where his work focused on high school graduation rates and the role of culture, student voice, and two-eyed seeing in increasing Indigenous student success.

Foreword

Vince Bustamante, Tim Cusack, and Wayne Davies have written a book that details strategies to support novice educators and encourage their successful transition into teaching. The school leader who recognizes the need for an effective and organized mentoring process yet must delegate the responsibility to an educator closer to the classroom will find this book especially beneficial. Concurrently, *The Mentor's Guidebook* serves the mentor who has achieved success as a teacher and wants to continue to grow and become exceptional in a supportive role. This kind of mentor is a committed lifelong learner who seeks enhanced professional development for personal improvement in addition to facilitating the growth of any teacher they mentor. Additionally, the mentor has genuine compassion for new teachers and understands that supporting them fosters their students' growth and their school's stability. Thus, the guidance offered in this book attends to the need of mentors' personal high expectations for their own continued success.

The authors create a clear path for mentors and school leaders who realize the importance of providing productive support during the induction phase of new teachers. They have written a manual for all educators who want to do significantly more than introduce a new teacher to the "location of the break room" and check in at the end of the year by asking, "How was your first year of teaching?" Moreover, the authors impart the skill of mentoring through their clear explanation and systemic organization of the process, all the while underscoring the commitment necessary to navigate the fluidity of effective and authentic relationships. This work has the potential to increase the number of teachers who remain in the field beyond the novice phase of teaching. We have seen the troubling statistic that only 1 out of 10 teachers recommend teaching and 52% of Black, Indigenous, and People of Color (BIPOC) teachers leave within the first two years, which undermines the stability and effectiveness of the profession and, most importantly, the needs of students. The authors identify the beneficiaries of their content to include all new teachers, including second-career professionals who enter the field and are sorely needed by our students. Our students can gain multiple new perspectives and skills from the experiences of educators who possess a variety of lived experiences and identities. All new teachers need mentors to help with the small tasks of teaching and the larger responsibility of creating inclusive and growth-producing instruction and classroom cultures. To be sure, for new teachers to effectively address the complexity our students require, teachers need to be mentored and authentically supported, to receive constructive feedback, and to celebrate wins that encourage their innate desire to continue to grow.

The authors reveal the reciprocity of mentorship as an opportunity to reflect on their own teaching practices and learn from the interaction with their mentee, thereby contributing to creating a transformational experience. Acknowledging the opportunity for mutual growth and ongoing self-awareness makes the reader aware that mentorship is not simply giving support to another teacher, but gaining a reciprocal learning opportunity for their own continued professional development and the demonstration of lifelong learning. Mentorship becomes its own reward for the courageous teacher committed to personal growth through reflective practices provided in the book. The authors provide unique perspectives and solutions to reciprocal learning and expand the capacity of schools to recruit effective mentors with the support from this book.

One opportunity for reciprocal learning and reflection is self-awareness, which is necessary for the mentor and mentee to develop a willingness to challenge personal assumptions and unconscious and self-serving biases. The foundation of the mentor's self-awareness and the synergy of reciprocal learning contributes to the mentor engaging the new and potentially exceptional teacher in experiencing the importance of self-awareness of the *attitudes*, *biases*, *conceptual understanding*, and *dispositions* of mentoring and teaching. The reflection of the mentor on their ABCDs creates the opportunity to invite the mentee to consider how their self-serving biases can impede their relationships with students, colleagues, and potentially the mentor. This practice of ongoing reflection on biases, which improves the classroom and school climate, can be a discussion between the mentor and mentee as they share their personal reflections and provide feedback to each other. Thus, with this book as a guide, the mentor and mentee gain opportunities to teach and share how they are learning through mentoring. Insights also encourage mentorship momentum through sustained progress in learning and growth encouraged by engagement, feedback, and goal-oriented actions.

The authors also communicate the importance of mastery of student learning. Teachers have multiple opportunities to consider the significance of their role in student learning through their teacher preparation program. The mentor's role is critical in helping the new teacher connect their actions to student success and may require an application of a synthesis of the strategies offered throughout this book. This particular focus is an opportunity to critique the perceptions of the mentor and mentee's biases about the student's capacity to learn and the teacher's capacity to identify and facilitate effective strategies to teach all students. Accordingly, another opportunity arises for the mentor and the teacher to examine perceptions and biases that influence the teacher's beliefs about the shared capacity of the teacher and student interaction.

Reading this book opened a dialogue I had with a new teacher, one who enthusiastically expressed her joy in her first year of teaching at the half-year mark. As we talked, her personal joy was tempered by her reflection that she knew she was having a unique experience. She was hired at the same school where she completed her student teaching; therefore, she was welcomed into a familiar place in which she had demonstrated success. However, she knew many of the new teachers in her cohort from college were not having similar positive experiences. When I asked her if she had a mentor, I was surprised to learn she did not. I could not help but wonder how a mentor as a part of her first year of teaching could support her enthusiasm for the remainder of the year and beyond.

I asked what she would want from an experience with a mentor, and not surprisingly, she mentioned experiences that the authors identify in this book. She mentioned the importance of building a relationship between herself and the mentor, "getting to know each other, sharing our pasts, experiences, specialties, and passions," and meeting at different locations such as coffee shops to support the authenticity of the relationship. She identified the need for a schedule for check-ins and to understand the purpose or focus of check-ins. The teacher stated the need for support in addressing her challenges, strengths, and aspirations; listening to her; advising her; and sharing resources that would push her to be a better educator. Additionally, she expressed the desire to have a mentor challenge her growth. As I casually analyzed her statements on what a mentor would do to support her, I noticed that Bustamante, Cusack, and Davies have written the strategies for mentor teachers through the framework of the Mentorship Mindset Model.

This is a teacher we need to see grow and remain in the profession with joy. Her enthusiasm and identity are needed by students and colleagues. I hope her excitement will continue for many years and be contagious to others.

An often-overlooked function for mentors that the authors highlight is intentionality in examining the policies and procedures of the school and strategies for working with all professionals in the school. Mentors can help "pull back the curtain" of what may be the stated policies of schools and the actual culture of the school. Concurrently, understanding the culture and the hierarchy of the school community supports the longevity and success of new teachers.

In a conversation with another first-year teacher who also didn't have a mentor, I learned that she had decided to leave the profession at the midyear mark because she neither understood the hierarchy of the school nor felt welcomed by the other teachers in the building. The authors identify this important aspect of creating success for new teachers. Without question, the new teacher I mentioned and many others I've encountered would be less inclined to leave if they had mentors to facilitate successful and encouraging experiences. The mentor can help new teachers develop relationships with existing teachers and educators and better navigate unspoken but existing cultures regarding the implementation of policies and the importance of developing effective communication with all educators in the school, some of whom serve in nonteaching roles.

In conclusion, as educators we all share the responsibility of supporting new teachers and encouraging experienced teachers who serve as mentors to grow and communicate the joy of teaching. *The Mentor's Guidebook: Unleashing Your Potential to Inspire and Retain New Teachers* contributes to the effective introduction of new teachers to the complexity of teaching and reclaims the narrative regarding the meaningful profession of teaching.

Dr. Franita Ware,
CEO of F Ware PhD Consulting LLC and Qualitative Data Analysis
Consultant with Innovative Learning Center LLC

Acknowledgments

From Vince Bustamante:

When I approached Tim and Wayne with the idea of simultaneously writing two books at the same time, they both excitedly agreed! Without them neither project would have been a success. In the case of this mentorship book project, I owe everything to them. They provided me with mentorship and guidance as we collaboratively worked to create a book that I am very proud of. Tim and Wayne, it was truly a pleasure sharing this space with both of you, and I look forward to our future collaboration.

When implemented effectively, mentorship can be an invaluable resource for both new and seasoned teachers. I extend my heartfelt gratitude to you, the reader, for choosing this text and for your dedication to enhancing our profession through the refinement of your craft. Whether you serve as a formal mentor or provide informal support to a colleague, your service is deeply appreciated.

I want to express my sincerest thanks to Dr. Franita Ware for including her voice in the foreword. Thank you, Franita, for the rich conversation, for the incredible perspective, and for your support of teachers everywhere. You truly are a gift to the profession.

Thank you to the Corwin family for your unwavering support for this project, and of me as an author. A special thank-you to Jessica Allan and the entire editorial team. I am appreciative of the collaborative approach to making this work truly the best it could possibly be. It is truly a privilege to have our work represented by Corwin, and I am excited for future opportunities.

Finally, and most importantly, my deepest gratitude goes to my wife, Leah. Your unwavering support, patience, and wisdom have been my anchor throughout this entire journey. As I navigated the challenges of yet another book project, your encouragement and guidance were the steady force that kept me moving forward. You are the backbone of our home, and without you, none of this would be possible. There is no doubt in my mind that this book would not have come to fruition without you by my side. For all that you do, and for the love and strength you bring to every day, I will forever be grateful. I am so excited for our future together with Luca and our new addition on the way.

From Timothy P. Cusack:

One of the best parts of writing this book with Vince and Wayne has been the opportunity to learn from them. It is remarkable to note that many of the mentoring techniques and processes we share in this book were inherent to how we collaborated in the writing process. Learning "from and with" others is central to our professional growth. The richness of dialogue, debate, and discussion is a treasured gift that I have received from this author team. Thank you!

Speaking of mentorship, I am thankful for the talented team at Corwin who have guided and shaped me as an author and consultant for almost five years now. I am thankful for the opportunity to share my professional knowledge and experience and relate it to the wider education community. I am also thankful to learn from the many thought leaders and champions of great teaching and learning within the Corwin family. Thank you!

I wish to thank my wife, Dr. Susan Coates, for her ongoing support and input into the important work of mentoring new teachers. She, like the many school and system leaders I have been blessed to serve alongside, reminds me of the moral imperative to do everything possible to best prepare our new teachers for the challenges and rewards ahead of them. Thank you!

Finally, I want to thank you, the reader of this book, for the important role you play in supporting and developing our early career teachers. Your work in serving as a mentor is truly central to creating the school culture and conditions that will encourage new teachers to thrive and remain within the profession. It is our sincerest hope that this book will help you to grow as a mentor and reinforce your passion and commitment to provide the best teaching and learning possible for our students. Thank you!

From Wayne Davies:

This book is the culmination of many months of thinking, writing, reflecting, and collaborating. My participation would not have been possible without the incredible support of numerous individuals and communities. To begin, I must express my deepest gratitude to my coauthors (who were also my mentors throughout this project), Vince and Tim. Your dedication, expertise, and unwavering commitment to the project have been instrumental in bringing this work to fruition, and I am indebted to you for your constant support, cooperation, and shared vision of assisting mentors in their important role of guiding new teachers. I look forward to working alongside you both on many more projects to come.

To my family, words cannot fully capture the depth of my appreciation for your love, support, and assistance throughout this journey. Tess, Kendall, and Clyde, you are my foundation. Your patience and belief in me have made it possible for me to pursue this work with confidence and dedication. Your unwavering encouragement has been a source of strength, and for that, I am forever grateful. To my greatest mentors, Lloyd and Peggy Davies, thank you. Through my actions as a teacher, leader, and mentor I have tried to reflect all that you instilled in me.

I am also deeply grateful to all the students, staff, and caregivers I have shared the road with over the years. Your stories and experiences have inspired and motivated me, and I have learned "much from many" as a former colleague used to say. I will forever cherish the opportunity to have worked in vastly varied environments and systems beginning with my time on the Lax Kw'alaams reserve with the Tsimshian First Nation and then eventually coming home to the prairies where I shared the journey with many incredible people including my greatest professional mentor, Dr. Christine Penner.

To my colleagues at the University of Winnipeg, thank you for providing me with numerous experiences, feedback, and stories that have guided my writing. The collaborative and intellectually stimulating environment you foster has played a pivotal role in shaping my thoughts and ideas on many topics. I am fortunate to work alongside such dedicated and thoughtful individuals who continually inspire me to be a better educator, researcher, and writer.

Finally, I would like to recognize the Corwin family for all the support and encouragement I have received during this project and over my time facilitating professional learning in a variety of school districts. The support each of you has shown me in my efforts to learn, grow, and contribute to the educational well-being of staff and students is greatly appreciated. Your dedication to helping everyone grow is outstanding and very well exemplified in how you made the writing of this book so enjoyable. I will forgo naming specific people, but you certainly know who you are and how much I thank you!

In closing, it is my sincere hope that this book serves as a small contribution to the ongoing work of supporting and empowering those who are shaping the next generation of educators and, by extension, learners. Thank you to you, the reader, for becoming part of my journey and allowing myself, Tim, and Vince to become part of yours.

PUBLISHER'S ACKNOWLEDGMENTS

Corwin gratefully acknowledges the contributions of the following reviewers:

Jennifer Abrams
Author, *Having Hard Conversations*
Palo Alto, California

Jacob Hollnagel
Educational Consultant, Wisconsin Department of Public Instruction
Minneapolis, Minnesota

Kirsten Olson

Introduction

SIGNS, SIGNS, EVERYWHERE THERE'S SIGNS

Help wanted. We have all seen these signs. Usually observed in the window of a corner store or restaurant, the appeal is for individuals to step up and step into a readily available employment opportunity. Whether we care to admit it or not, help wanted signs could easily be displayed at schools. Simply stated, we need more individuals to step up and step into teaching. Given the current realities of the teaching landscape, which are well publicized in research and by the media, there is a "teacher shortage." The shortage is not simply a teacher acquisition issue. We argue that it is more so, a retention problem.

According to recent statistics, if we were to visit a staff room in the United States consisting of 100 teachers, this is what we might observe: 55 will retire or leave the profession prematurely (Jotkoff, 2022; Walker, 2021); 33 are likely to leave teaching in the next two years (Will, 2023); 42 do not feel respected by the public (Gallup, 2024); 39 feel burned out (Gallup, 2024); and only 16 would recommend the profession of teaching to a young adult (Educators for Excellence, 2024). Our hope in writing this book is to help reclaim and reframe the narrative of what it means to be a teacher today. The preceding statistics are staggering, but do not lose heart. We know more can be done to help prepare the teachers we so urgently need. We want *at least 9 out of 10 teachers to recommend this career* and support those who are seeking to make this a lifelong endeavor. The only way we can reclaim and reframe the narrative is with *your help*. By picking up this book, you are becoming part of the solution regardless of where you currently find yourself. You are the help we need to retain our new and aspiring teachers, and by sharing your experiences and expertise you will be a part of the solution and not part of the existing narrative.

Who Is This Book for? It's for You!

Whether you were tapped on the shoulder, you reluctantly agreed, or you raised your hand high in the air and said, "I would love to serve as a mentor," you have found your way to this book. Your role in helping another teacher to grow and develop is essential to being part of the solution to retain early career teachers. It is possible that you might not have a lot of background or training in how to be a more effective mentor. That is OK. Do not worry. We've got you covered. We are going to walk you through some of the key concepts of how to not just feel like a better mentor but be a better mentor! If you do have experience as a mentor, we invite you to reinforce your existing skills and experience by tagging along and challenging your assumptions (as well as ours) in exploring what makes for a good mentoring environment.

Being asked (or told) to serve as a mentor is an honor but can also be daunting. Often, we may not have depth of practical experience with mentoring. If you have been shoulder tapped or even volunteered (been "volun-told") to take on a new teacher by serving as their mentor, this book is for you. While many jurisdictions offer a measure of formal mentorship, the depth of programming and resources may vary. Our goal with this book is to help better equip you to be a great mentor to an early career teacher.

Over the course of our careers, we may become responsible for supporting newer teachers regardless of whether we are "officially" called a mentor or not. Whether we are given a new teacher or have inherited a new colleague in our school, the reality is that our profession thrives on more experienced individuals sharing their knowledge and expertise with newer teachers. "Unofficial" or "informal" mentors are critical to the success of our new and budding teachers. You provide a friendly face, a partner who is working alongside them, or a person who is immediately accessible (this is especially true when working in larger school districts).

Research suggests that informal mentorship relationships significantly contribute to teacher professional development and job satisfaction (Hobson, 2002; Ingersoll & Kralik, 2004). Unlike formal mentorship programs, which may be limited in scope or availability, unofficial mentors offer personalized assistance tailored to the specific needs of mentees, fostering a sense of camaraderie and community within the teaching profession (Johnson, 2019). Therefore, recognizing and fostering unofficial mentorship in teaching can enhance teacher retention, improve instructional quality, and ultimately benefit student learning outcomes. Our hope is that you see value in this book to support you as you assist the new teachers in your school.

If only 16% of current teachers recommend becoming a teacher, it does not take long to realize that the very people we are hoping will serve as mentors and coaches for the next generation of teachers are more likely to steer aspiring teachers away. Given that 86% of school boards in the United States are facing hiring challenges and only 43% of teachers under the age of 30 indicate they plan to make teaching a career (Gallup, 2024), the education workforce is likely to diminish. Again, this is not just a problem in the United States; it is prevalent in Canada and around the world.

In the fall of 2023, several Canadian provinces indicated shortages. British Columbia, Ontario, and Quebec signaled a need to increase the number of new teachers available. The Ontario College of Teachers (2020) noted that between 2008 and 2011 there were 7,788 more teachers entering the profession compared to those retiring. In 2012–2014, the annual difference was 5,170. From 2015 to 2018 it was 1,898. Fast-forward to 2019–2022 and the annual difference is 193. The number of new teachers coming into the profession is quickly approaching equilibrium with the number of teachers who are retiring.

It is not just Canada and the United States that are facing the need to attract and retain more new teachers. For World Teachers' Day in October 2023 the theme was "The teachers we need for the education we want: The global imperative to reverse the teacher shortage." There is a global shortage of teachers! Consider these statistics raised at the conference and in a 2022 UNESCO report:

- Significant teacher shortages are still prevalent in many low-income countries, specifically in sub-Saharan Africa, whereby 5.4 million teachers at the primary level and 11.1 million teachers at the secondary level are needed to achieve the targets set for 2030.
- Teacher shortages in Australia have resulted in the employment of unqualified science, technology, engineering, and mathematics (STEM) teachers.

Consider this statement from Teacher Education Specialist Dr. Betty Ogange (2023): "Rural and disadvantaged communities are particularly hard hit, as they lack both the numbers and the calibre of teachers needed for quality education. The ripple effect of this shortage is enormous, exacerbating social divides and hindering progress toward global sustainability goals." Clearly the need to attract and retain teachers is a universal matter that requires clear, targeted, and strategic action.

Another Perspective

As we mentioned at the outset, we do not want to overstate the perceived teacher shortage problem, nor are we trying to be dramatic by exclaiming "the sky is falling." Consider a counter perspective:

There is no teacher shortage. There's a teacher recruitment and retention problem. There's a "making the job attractive enough to draw in the people we want" problem. There is a problem that requires a careful, thoughtful diagnosis. There are policy and political leaders who see the current situation as an opportunity to be exploited rather than a problem to be solved. (Greene, 2022)

PAUSE AND REFLECT I.1

What do you think about this perspective? Is it more of a recruitment and retention problem than an actual shortage? What else comes to mind when you read this quote?

Every year we, as a profession, collectively welcome thousands of new teachers. They are excited, well trained, and as ready as they can be to take on the role of professional educator. Fast-forward five years and a significant number have prematurely left the profession. The reasons for this untimely exit are numerous and not always immediately apparent. Some were unable to land in positions that made them feel they could make the contribution they wanted, while others were overwhelmed by the demands of the career. Perhaps they did not have a mentor who helped them make sense of what they were being confronted with, or maybe they were unable to find like minds and other new teachers in the same position with whom to share their wonderings or frustrations.

Either way, it is clear that if we do not stem the tide and slow the flow of teachers leaving the profession prematurely, we will continue in a loop of too few trying to do too much, resulting in more early leaving and perpetuation of this vicious cycle. The more new teachers there are who can find their stride and stay, the more support there will be for others to do the same. You are always spiraling; the key is to be spiraling up!

So what to do? To suggest major policy shifts or propose funding increases is beyond our jurisdiction. Thus, we will choose to stay in our sphere of control and suggest instead that a fulsome effort to support new teachers by helping them access mentors as well as link up with colleagues who are similar in experience is a large part of the answer. The more collaborative the culture, the stronger the feeling of belonging to a team with high collective efficacy.

If we can help these emerging professionals focus on the joy of the job and find supports from more experienced educators around them to flatten some of the learning curve, and then we allow them to figure out what they need to succeed with "like minds," we will see teachers thrive past the "first five" and become seasoned veterans in this most amazing of professions.

Recalling the statistics we shared near the opening of this introduction, we know that many teachers indicate they want to leave the profession within the next two to five years (Jotkoff, 2022; Walker, 2021). We also know that 52% of Black, Indigenous, and People of Color (BIPOC) teachers will leave within the first two years (Gallup, 2024). We also note that only 1 in 10 teachers would recommend the profession to a young adult still considering a career path (Educators for Excellence, 2024). The reasons for leaving are often complicated and situational in nature, but that does not discount the amount of new, qualified teachers leaving the profession with a distaste for the practice that we love.

There is one statistic, however, that gives us great hope. According to *Education Week* (Will, 2023), two out of every three teachers feel some measure of satisfaction in their work. These are the two-thirds we are hoping will want to share that spark, those moments of joy and wonder, with new teachers. These are the teachers we hope will read this book and learn new ways to help ignite and kindle the flames of passion and resilience for great teaching and learning. Given that you are reading this book, we want to take a moment to say thank you and reinforce how important it is for you to serve as a mentor to an early career teacher.

If we are going to navigate our way to better teacher preparation, onboarding, and ultimately retention, we need you (the mentor) to be part of the solution. Through this book, we want to showcase how we can be even more intentional and deliberate in how we prepare our mentor teachers. We want to better equip you to be an even better mentor so that the impact you have on new teachers is not only circumstantial but also sustainable. So what is in this endeavor for you and your school? Journey with us as we help guide you to come to a deeper understanding of your attitudes, biases, conceptual understanding, and dispositions about mentorship. We will share an array of mentorship approaches and offer practical ways for you to engage more capably and confidently with your mentees.

Why Mentorship?

Why are we so passionate about mentorship? As evidenced by the following collection of research, effective mentoring improves teacher retention, enhances instructional practices, boosts confidence, supports professional development, and contributes to better student outcomes. Furthermore, mentorship fosters a positive and collaborative school culture, helping to address specific challenges in diverse classrooms. Therefore, mentorship is a crucial strategy for ensuring the long-term success and well-being of new teachers, as well as the academic success of their students. According to the Alberta Teachers' Association (2024) longitudinal study of over 5,000 early career teachers, mentorship was identified as the number-one ask (Gunn & McRae, 2024). Other complementary research identifies the following benefits of a mentorship program:

- **Improves teacher retention:** A study by Ingersoll and Strong (2011) found that teachers who participated in formal mentoring programs were more likely to stay in the profession compared to those who did not receive mentorship. Specifically, the study indicated that new teachers who received strong mentoring had a 30%–50% higher retention rate after the first five years of teaching compared to those who did not.
- **Increases sense of preparedness:** We have known for some time now that one of the most significant predictors of teacher retention is their sense of preparedness (Darling-Hammond et al., 2002) to engage in the fundamental tasks of teaching and learning. Quality engagement with a mentor teacher, especially for preservice teachers, can increase their sense of efficacy and perception of readiness and preparedness in their practicum experiences (Curtis et al., 2019). This supports greater levels of retention (Gunn & McRae, 2021, 2024).
- **Increases teacher effectiveness:** In a study by Keller-Schneider et al. (2020), novice teachers who were paired with experienced mentors showed significant improvement in their teaching practices. Observations indicated that teachers with mentorship support were more adept at adapting instruction to meet students' diverse needs and were better at creating engaging learning environments.

- **Enhances teacher confidence and well-being:** According to Chesley and Jordan (2012), mentorship has a positive impact on teachers' psychological well-being. Their study found that teachers with mentors reported lower levels of stress, higher levels of job satisfaction, and greater self-efficacy. This was particularly true for teachers who faced challenging classroom environments or those in underresourced schools.
- **Addresses specific challenges in diverse classrooms:** According to a study by Van Bergen and colleagues (2020), mentorship programs tailored to new teachers in diverse or low-income schools were highly effective in helping teachers manage issues like student behavior, language barriers, and cultural responsiveness. The mentors in these programs were able to share specific strategies for working with diverse learners, which helped increase the new teachers' sense of competence.

Our Perspective

The authors of this book are teachers. We have each experienced our own unique entry to the profession and subsequently mentored numerous other aspiring teachers. With experience in school leadership and system leadership and current leadership roles in postsecondary teacher preparation and instructional consulting, we bring a variety of knowledge and experience to this book. More than this, we have woven the voices of aspiring teachers and active mentors into the discussions, providing you with a chance to hear them share practical, usable solutions and strategies, a cornerstone of what this book is built upon.

We firmly believe that by having a better understanding of the needs from the field and that by better equipping our mentor teachers with the "how" of being a great mentor, we can collectively engage our new and emerging teachers in more authentic and encouraging ways. We want to do more than just help you retain teachers; we want to help you equip them to persevere and find joy and success in serving the educational needs of children. We believe, with this book, we can assist in creating the optimal conditions necessary for successful mentorship that will result in more teachers wanting to enter, remain, and thrive in what we believe is the greatest profession!

Why Mentorship Is Important to Us

Vince Bustamante: Best-Selling Author and Consultant

When I first started in my teaching career, I was mentorless. Starting in a school halfway through a school year lends itself to complications when it comes to being the "new guy." It was a rough half year, and at the end I found myself questioning whether this was the right career for me. Luckily, the following school year I was "adopted" by one of my assistant principals who made it his goal to impart his knowledge and priorities onto me. He invested time and encouraged me to explore my impact on the classroom environment and my instructional capacity. If it wasn't for him, I would have left the profession. It is due to this experience I found myself longing to support and mentor new teachers, ensuring they are aware of the uniqueness and importance of their roles in the lives of their students.

I am passionate about mentoring new teachers to make an impact both inside and outside the walls of their classroom—about establishing an environment where students can truly be their unique selves, and can learn in a place where rigor is important but multiple attempts at mastery are more important. Regardless of the grade we teach, all students deserve a teacher who shows up for their students, and in turn our new teachers deserve us to show up for them as mentors.

Tim Cusack: Award-Winning Principal, Former Superintendent, Dean of Education, and Naval Warfare Officer

When I trained to be a teacher, my university preparation program provided the basic building blocks needed, but it would be in my first few formative years of teaching in rural Alberta where I would cut my teaching teeth. I did not have the benefit of a formal mentor but was able to glean a balance of *what to do* and also *what not to do* through working with and observing other teachers. What I did have was the benefit of earlier career training in the Royal Canadian Navy. It would be elements of leadership development and military approaches to mentorship that gave me a leg up in terms of not just surviving but eventually thriving in my teaching practice. Without that mix of formal and informal mentorship, I likely would not have stayed five years in a small rural northern community. Eventually, I moved into assistant principalship, principalship, and superintendency, where I developed a deep desire and passion to build the self- and collective efficacy of teachers. I wanted to build supports and structures that would entice teachers to stay, grow, and flourish in their practice. This eventually led to my doctoral studies, which focused on mentorship and creating conditions that help better prepare aspiring leaders.

I firmly believe that teachers are leaders. They lead learning and the learning community that is their classroom. When I had the opportunity to become dean of education and serve teacher preparation programming, I knew I wanted to help to better prepare early career teachers for the current and forthcoming challenges facing K–12 today. Further, I want to support mentor teachers to feel more capable and confident in welcoming and working with new teachers. More intentionality in this regard is central to my experience and passion to help teachers mentor teachers and, ultimately, create rich and vibrant learning environments for students.

Wayne Davies: Nationally Recognized School Leader, Consultant, and Author

Simply put, my reason for contributing to the writing of this book is that after 30 or so years of working in schools as a teacher and leader, I know we can do a better job giving our colleagues a great start to their careers. This belief is doubly so for new teachers from equity-seeking and racialized groups. Student bodies are changing quickly, and so too, albeit not as quickly, is the composition of teaching staffs.

Every hire should reflect the very best efforts to put the best possible teacher in front of students. This requires effort and resources, both valuable commodities in this fast-paced, demanding world. Finding talented people who are qualified and ready to put in the time and energy necessary to help students succeed is important. Just as important is continuing efforts and putting resources forward to support and retain these teachers to allow them to take flight and succeed over the long term in their classrooms.

When it comes to equity-seeking and racialized teachers just beginning their teaching journeys, it is even more important as they take on the added work of equity and inclusion within their buildings. These teachers will be asked to do things that many of their colleagues will not. They will be asked to work on school projects such as Martin Luther King Jr. Day, Black History Month, Truth and Reconciliation Commission initiatives, and a myriad of others. They will be the ones who get asked to speak at assemblies, to talk in their peers' classrooms, and to help navigate and explain the issues the school wrestles with to their peers and the greater community. Some will feel the pressure of being "the" role model whether they want to be or not. They will need support to do this work. Thus, I am called to assist in writing this book to help all of us navigate the work that providing mentorship represents, a chance for all of us to grow, to be better together.

Mentorship Mindset

So what sets this book apart from other books on how to be a better mentor to an early career teacher? We propose a model that, regardless of whether you have existing mentorship skills and background or are brand new to the role of being a mentor, will guide you to deepening your confidence, competency, and impact. Just because you may have participated in your school or district's formal or informal mentorship program does not necessarily mean that more cannot be done to increase your skills and effectiveness as a mentor. Whereas the composition and content of mentorship training programs varies, there are some key mentorship components that need to be front and center in the preparation provided. We affectionately refer to the combination of these components as the Mentorship Mindset Model. It is a way of thinking about and enacting approaches to mentoring early career teachers that will help you sharpen your skills in practical ways. As you will observe in Figure I.1, there are five areas of focus:

1. **Motivation**: What are your motivations (intentions) in serving as a mentor and taking training to learn more about how to be an effective mentor for an early career teacher? Is taking on a mentee simply one more thing you "have to do" or "get to do"? Are you genuinely interested in developing the skills of a new teacher?
2. **Modality**: What is your level of comfort, capability, confidence, and credibility as a mentor? What do you need to help you grow as a more effective mentor for early career teachers?
3. **Matching**: To what extent, if any, does your program focus on understanding "fit"? That is, how intentional is the pairing of mentor and mentee? Is there a discernment process, or is it more "luck of the draw"? What perceived hierarchical structures or power dynamics (or imbalances) might be in play? How do you navigate this?
4. **Momentum**: How much time do you have to commit to the mentorship program? Being an impactful teacher requires much of your time and attention, but adding the mentorship layer increases demands on your time. What release time or other school (district) supports are in place to support the time you need to serve as a mentor? What routines and practices move your mentorship meetings forward?

Figure I.1 • Mentorship Mindset Model

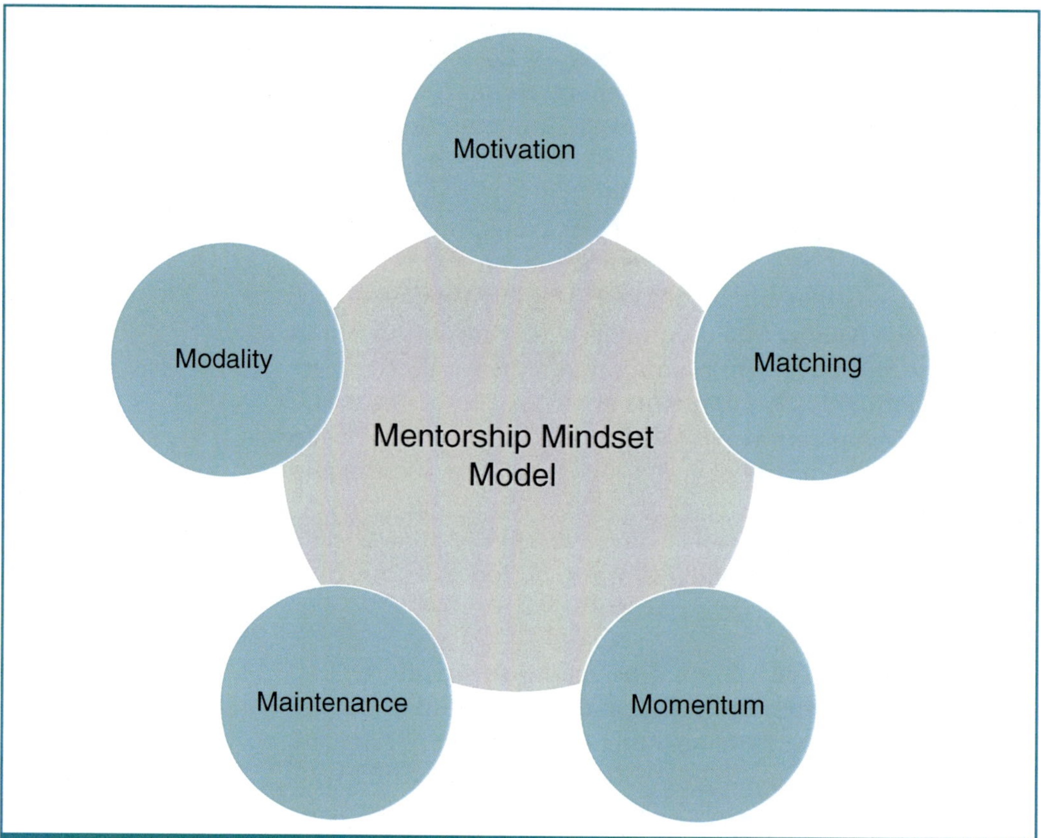

5. **Maintenance:** There are often factors such as job security (of the mentee), drastic changes of assignments (placements) for early career teachers, changes in roles for the mentor, and other intangibles that can disrupt fledgling or well-established mentoring pairings (groups). How might you handle the elements of change or disruption that can impact mentoring? How do you nurture, grow, and celebrate successes along the journey?

In Chapters 1 through 3, we will explore aspects of motivation, modality, and matching. Think of it as Part I of the book. This first half of the guidebook will have two recurring features to help you better understand "what you think about mentoring and how to mentor." We will first venture into the *attitudes* we have about mentoring, the *biases* we might have about mentoring, our *conceptual understanding* of mentoring, and our *dispositions* toward mentoring others. We affectionately refer to these as the ABCDs of mentoring. Once we spend some time unpacking the ABCDs, we are going to share a mentorship model with you that will point you toward effective strategies and considerations on "how to mentor." We will examine *traditional* methods of mentoring that are known to be impactful. We will explore *interdependent* approaches to mentoring that empower learning from and with your mentee. We will spend some time thinking about how we think about mentoring with some *metacognitive* strategies, and finally, we will examine *environmental* (and cultural) factors that are essential to a thriving mentorship experience. We bring these four approaches together in what we call the T.I.M.E. approach to mentoring. So, equipped with the knowledge and insights of your ABCDs, we will spend some T.I.M.E. (pun intended) to understand how our feelings toward serving as a mentor can be channeled more effectively to become a more effective and impactful mentor to an early career teacher. Trust us when we say this will be as easy as ABCD and time well spent!

What we also want to note about these mentorship components is the important role that school (and district) leadership has in helping create the conditions for you to find more success as a mentor. There are many factors involved in creating effective mentorship training programs beyond a course, or a professional development session, or a book. We want you to know that just as "it takes a village to raise a child," it takes the entire school's teacher and support staff community (your school village per se) to help raise an early career teacher.

The second half of the book (Part II) will focus on hands-on, practical ways to help you move forward with your mentee. These will include how to develop a growth mindset, how to communicate with all members of the learning community, and how to adapt to change, which sometimes occurs suddenly! Chapter 4 takes the relationship and discussion level deeper as mentor–mentee conversations turn to engagement and preparation and what to do when the best laid plans do not go as planned! Insights on how to recognize small signs of problems before they grow larger will be shared, as will how to assist mentees in finding the right balance when it comes to extracurricular and faculty work. Chapter 5 wraps up by highlighting the more joyous and rewarding part of the career. This includes a discussion on how teachers are in a unique position to weave their passions and interests into the work they do with students, opening their minds to possibilities and opportunities otherwise unconsidered. Of course, throughout the book perspectives of "real" mentors and mentees are shared along with a variety of tools and concepts that will add value to your work as a mentor.

To summarize our perspectives and the purpose of this book, we truly care about teaching and the new teachers who are joining us in this esteemed profession. It is our hope that through your journey you learn about yourself as not only a teacher, but also a mentor, so that you can share your experiences and expertise with the next generation of teachers. High-quality teachers breed high-quality teaching when they share their expertise with mentees who are looking for a trusted colleague to guide them through the tumultuous first few months and years in the classroom.

CHAPTER ONE

Who Are You as a Mentor?

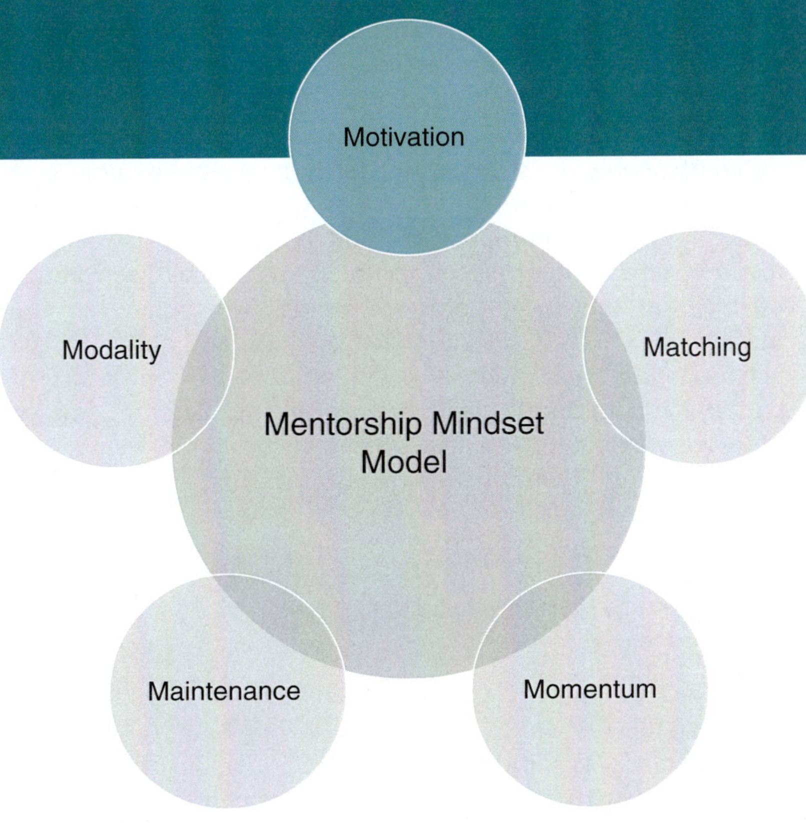

To be a mentor you need to understand what's going on in a young person's life and you just want to have an internal dialogue that says, "How can I help? Because I really care."

— Deepak Chopra (see Mentoring Complete, 2014)

MENTOR: WHAT DOES IT MEAN?

Before we can launch into this book about how to become a better mentor, we first need to understand the word itself. The term *mentor* has become so commonplace in education and other disciplines and is so nuanced in meaning that it becomes fuzzy or blurry as to what it really means. We know that the etymology of *mentor* is Greek, meaning "wise and trusted." From Homer's *Odyssey* (8th century BCE/2003), we recall that Mentor was a friend of Odysseus and served as a tutor (a more knowledgeable other) to Telemachus. Thus, in a classical sense, when we hear the word *mentor*, we think of synonyms such as *teacher*, *guide*, *advisor*, *master*, *coach*, *champion*, *guru*, and the like.

When we think of the many attributes and qualities associated with being a mentor, the sheer scope of the word *mentor* diffuses even more. Is a mentor a guide? A critical friend? A role model? Essentially, the word means many things to many different people. In many ways the term *mentor* is more of a label that encompasses the many acts of support we provide others. What is common, however, is that, in some way, a mentor helps another person to learn. This is what we want to establish as our focal point. Moreover, we argue that the mentor seeks to raise the knowledge, skills, and ability of the person being mentored. We will address this in terms of building and guiding the self-efficacy of others later on, but for now, we want you to surface your own thoughts, views, and understanding of what being a mentor means.

THE "WHO" BEFORE WE DO

Think back to a time in your life when you were learning something for the first time. Was it easy to do? Did you struggle? Likely, there was a more knowledgeable person present supporting you with the task or concept. A parent, teacher, or close friend perhaps? Would you consider that person to have been a mentor to you? We hear the word *mentor* a lot in education, but it is a word that is often taken for granted. What do we mean by this? Just because someone with more experience, wisdom, or lived practice shows us how to learn something new, it does not necessarily mean that they are serving in the capacity of a mentor. Being a mentor, as Deepak

Chopra clarifies (see Mentoring Complete, 2014), requires entering a relationship with someone who not only needs to learn or be developed but *wants* to learn and develop. We will unpack this in greater detail soon, but first, let's think about the individuals we might consider as being our mentor(s).

If you were to make a list of all the people in your professional context who served as a mentor to you, how many names would there be? Were they seasoned teachers, school leaders, or system leaders? Beyond that, what characteristics, attributes, and approaches to the teaching, learning, and assessment inherent to their mentoring stood out for you? Most likely, you will suggest there was a strong relationship between you and your mentor. Your mentor knew how and when to push and challenge you and when to ease off. Your mentor was a cheerleader, motivator, and champion of your success. The positive mentorship attributes on your list are most likely to be the ones you would choose to emulate if you were serving as a mentor to someone.

Conversely, there are people in our professional encounters that we learn from but would not consider to be mentors. Have you ever experienced a situation and thought to yourself, "I'm pretty sure I wouldn't do it that way." Clearly, we can learn *what not to do* just as readily as we can learn *what to do*. If most of our mentorship experiences have been skewed to the *what not to do* side, our willingness to learn and take on new challenges becomes stymied. Negative role models (we call them tormentors) can leave a lingering, damaging effect—especially on our early career teachers. Given the pressures we discussed in the introduction about the need to attract and retain teachers, we cannot afford to have tormentors. Thus, in this book we will provide a practical approach to help you, an experienced classroom teacher, become the powerful, positive, caring "super-mentor" you have always wanted to be! How? We're glad you asked.

We know through social cognitive learning theory (SCLT) that we model our own actions and responses to stimuli after those individuals we look up to as an example. Bandura (1989) proposed that learning occurs through observation, imitation, and modeling. Our learning is influenced by factors such as attention, motivation, attitudes, and emotions. These predispositions to learning are important for a mentor to know. If we are going to meet our learner—in this case the pre- or early service teacher we are taking under our wing—where they are at, we need to have a rich sense of our own *attitudes, biases, conceptual understanding,* and *dispositions* toward mentorship. We call these the ABCDs of mentoring. Let's take a few moments to unpack these.

A IS FOR ATTITUDES

Your attitude refers to your mental and emotional stance or outlook on mentorship. It includes your feelings, beliefs, and values regarding the importance of mentorship, your expectations for the process, and how you perceive your role. In other words, attitude is more about your immediate reaction to being a mentor, and it's shaped by your personal experiences, outlook, and assumptions. For example:

- **Positive Attitude:** A mentor with a positive attitude might see mentorship as an opportunity to give back, build relationships, and help shape the future of education. They are likely to approach challenges with patience and a growth mindset, seeing setbacks as learning experiences.
- **Neutral or Negative Attitude:** A mentor with a less favorable attitude might view the role as burdensome or as an additional task, rather than a rewarding opportunity. They may be less motivated to engage deeply or consistently with the mentee.

In general, a mentor's attitude will influence the level of enthusiasm, empathy, and encouragement they provide to their mentee, as well as how they navigate challenges or setbacks in the mentorship process.

Attitude refers to a settled way of thinking or feeling about something (mindset), often reflected in a person's behavior. It encompasses an individual's outlook, beliefs, and feelings toward specific aspects of life or situations. Attitudes can influence how someone responds to challenges, interacts with others, and approaches tasks. They are often shaped by experiences, values, and perceptions, and can significantly affect one's effectiveness in various roles, including professional and personal contexts.

We know that mentors play a crucial role in guiding a new teacher through their early experiences in the classroom.

Here are five key attitudes that are particularly valuable for a mentor to embody:

- **Empathy:** Understanding the challenges and uncertainties that come with being a new teacher is essential. By showing empathy, a mentor can offer support that is both compassionate and practical, helping the new teacher navigate their initial hurdles and feel valued.
- **Patience:** Transitioning into teaching can be overwhelming. A mentor with patience will allow the new teacher to grow at their own pace, offering guidance and feedback without rushing or applying undue pressure.
- **Openness:** Being open to new ideas and methods can foster a positive learning environment. A mentor who embraces innovative approaches and listens to the new teacher's perspectives encourages creativity and professional growth.
- **Encouragement:** Providing positive reinforcement and acknowledging the new teacher's successes builds confidence and morale. Encouragement helps the new teacher to overcome setbacks and stay motivated.
- **Reflective Practice:** A mentor who engages in reflective practice models a growth mindset. By openly discussing what works well and what could be improved, the mentor helps the new teacher develop their own reflective habits, enhancing their teaching practice over time.

B IS FOR BIASES

Biases are preconceived notions or preferences that affect how we perceive and judge people, situations, or information. They often lead to unfair or skewed evaluations and can be based on stereotypes, personal experiences, or societal influences. Biases can impact decision making and behavior, sometimes without our conscious awareness.

While mentoring is a valuable and supportive practice in education, it's important to be aware of potential biases that may impact the mentoring process. Biases can unintentionally affect the mentor–mentee relationship and the guidance provided. Some common biases associated with mentoring teachers include the following:

- **Affinity Bias:** The tendency to favor people who share similar interests, backgrounds, or experiences to oneself

- **Confirmation Bias:** The tendency to seek, interpret, and remember information in a way that confirms one's pre-existing beliefs or assumptions
- **Generational Bias:** The tendency to favor or discriminate against people based on their age or the generation to which they belong
- **Status Quo Bias:** The preference for the current state of affairs and the tendency to resist changes from that baseline
- **Stereotype Bias:** The tendency to hold oversimplified and generalized beliefs about a particular group of people, often leading to prejudiced attitudes and discriminatory behavior

To address these biases, it's crucial for mentors and mentees to engage in open and honest communication. Mentors should actively seek diverse perspectives, be aware of their own biases, and strive to create an inclusive and equitable mentoring environment. Additionally, mentoring programs can implement training and guidelines to raise awareness about biases and promote fair and unbiased mentoring practices.

PAUSE AND REFLECT 1.1

Of the *attitudes* listed earlier, which ones are resonating with you most? Which ones do you think might require more time and attention on your part?

How might the manner in which you were mentored *bias* how you would mentor an early career teacher?

C IS FOR CONCEPTUAL UNDERSTANDING

Conceptual understanding refers to the awareness and recognition of abstract ideas and principles that underpin our knowledge and practice. It involves grasping the broader concepts and frameworks that shape a particular field or situation (in this case mentoring new teachers), beyond just the concrete details or surface-level information. In essence, it's the ability to see and comprehend the larger patterns, theories, and relationships that guide and influence specific phenomena or practices.

Mentoring teachers involves several key concepts that contribute to the effectiveness of the mentoring process. These concepts are fundamental to creating a supportive and growth-oriented relationship between mentors and mentees. Here are some key concepts associated with mentoring teachers:

- **Collaborative Learning:** An educational approach where individuals work together in groups to achieve a common goal, sharing knowledge and skills to enhance learning outcomes
- **Differentiated Support:** Providing tailored assistance and resources to individuals based on their specific needs, abilities, and learning styles to help them achieve their goals
- **Feedback and Assessment:** Evaluating performance or understanding and providing constructive comments to guide improvement and measure progress
- **Trust Building:** A process of establishing and nurturing mutual confidence and reliability between individuals or groups through consistent actions and communication
- **Reflective Practice:** The process of thoughtfully analyzing one's actions and experiences to continuously improve personal and professional effectiveness

These key concepts collectively contribute to the establishment of a positive mentoring environment that promotes continuous learning, collaboration, and the overall professional development of teachers.

D IS FOR DISPOSITIONS

Unlike your attitude, your disposition refers to your more grounded, enduring characteristics and natural tendencies as a mentor. It's your overall behavioral orientation and the kind of mentor you are inclined to be, shaped by your personality, temperament, and values. A person's disposition tends to reflect *how they act* in relation to mentorship over time, rather than just how they feel about it in the moment.

For instance:

- **Supportive Disposition:** A mentor with a naturally supportive disposition might consistently offer guidance, encouragement, and constructive feedback in a way that builds trust and confidence. Their demeanor is calm and reassuring, and they demonstrate patience and understanding.
- **Critical or Directive Disposition:** A mentor with a more directive disposition might prefer to take a more authoritative or solution-focused approach, providing specific instructions and expectations. They may prioritize efficiency and standards over nurturing relationships or building a sense of autonomy in the mentee.

While a mentor's attitude can shift based on context or specific situations, their disposition is more likely to remain consistent, as it reflects deeper-seated aspects of personality and approach to teaching and mentoring.

Dispositions are crucial because they shape how individuals engage with their roles, respond to challenges, and contribute to the learning environment. Positive dispositions in educators, for example, can significantly enhance their effectiveness and create a more supportive and productive classroom atmosphere.

The dispositions of a mentor play a critical role in the success of mentoring relationships, especially when working with early career or new teachers (including teachers from other countries). Here are key mentor dispositions associated with mentoring new teachers:

- **Active Listening:** Fully concentrating, understanding, responding, and remembering what is being said, demonstrating genuine interest and empathy in the conversation
- **Providing Constructive Feedback:** Offering feedback that is specific, actionable, and aimed at fostering growth and improvement, while maintaining a supportive and respectful approach
- **Championing Cultural Competence:** Actively promoting and practicing understanding, respect, and effective interaction with individuals from diverse cultural backgrounds
- **Promoting Lifelong Learners:** Continuously seeking and acquiring knowledge, skills, and experiences

throughout one's life to adapt to change and achieve personal and professional growth

- **Providing a Positive Outlook (broker of hope):** Consistently offering encouragement, optimism, and constructive perspectives to uplift and motivate others in various situations

By embodying these mentor dispositions, mentors can create a supportive and constructive mentoring environment that facilitates the growth and development of new teachers as they embark on their educational journey.

PAUSE AND REFLECT 1.2

Which of the *conceptual understanding* and *dispositions* of mentoring provided do you do well already? Which one or two might you wish to explore further?

YOUR CRITICAL ROLE AS A MENTOR

Think back to your days as a beginning teacher. How was your experience transitioning into this wonderful career? What were your first few days and weeks like as you took your initial steps into teaching? Did you go home at night with more questions than answers? Did you feel like you were constantly interrupting your colleagues, asking how to use the photocopier or where the first staff meeting would be? When that first report card writing period came around, were you dead sure you knew how to write great comments, submit them on time, and then get all your parent meetings booked? Or did you lie awake the night before, just hoping to survive it, wishing there was someone to talk to?

Maybe someone saw you looking a bit confused at the staff meeting, dropped by your classroom afterward, and offered you a few helpful pointers. Or perhaps the school leader assigned you a "mentor" who showed you around the building, got you a school coffee mug, and then checked in on you again in June to see if you had survived the year or not. It is also quite possible you had a very fulsome and robust experience and still keep in touch with the person who made a difference for you (Ingersoll & Strong, 2011). Thus, as you approach this relationship, you will need to surface and reflect on your own experiences and feelings about mentoring so that you can either go beyond what you experienced or use your past as a guide to also do a great job!

Whether or not you had a great experience, one thing is clear: You have been selected to be a mentor, and your mentee is excited to work with you! New teachers entering schools today are definite in their desire to be mentored. These new teachers view mentoring as a valuable part of their development and work. To add to this, the capacity of a school to offer formalized mentoring greatly helps schools attract and retain new teachers, especially Millennials and Gen Z. Research points to improved retention of emerging teachers. Considering we are in an era that is witnessing larger attrition than years past, with over half (55%) of those in the field considering leaving the profession, efforts to retain are more important than ever (Walker, 2022a, 2022b).

But why are you important as a mentor? You are important because you can help an emerging professional navigate the first months or years of what many of us know to be the greatest career in the world. You are important because you can use your expertise, your lived experiences, and your professional knowledge to help new teachers successfully navigate their way through their early years. Mentor selection is an important part of a successful mentorship program (Callahan, 2016). You can help build their confidence while seeing them through the most challenging time of their career. You can build their ability to self-reflect. You can position them for success, showing them ways to see opportunity in the chaos that can exist all around us in schools. You can be the one to show them the joy in their chosen profession.

How about those second-career teachers—why are you important to them? Maybe you can help them recognize that all those years as an entrepreneur have given them the skills necessary for successful teaching. Maybe you can help ease them through the awkwardness they might be feeling as a 40-year-old rookie. Starting over is never easy, but you can definitely make it "less hard."

The internationally trained teacher who just arrived in your community could surely use a hand navigating some of the informal customs and protocols your school follows. Maybe they could also use a tip on where the best restaurants are or just be introduced around to start gaining a sense of "home" again. At the same time, you might see an opportunity for reverse mentoring. Maybe they can strengthen your teaching with some advice on that science lab you just can't seem to make work while you talk to them about differentiation and assessment or whatever else they might be interested in. Do not be afraid to ask them questions too.

Yes, all of these are the reasons that you are important as a mentor: your patience, your enthusiasm, your humanity—the ability to make people feel good about things, about being new or starting over. You have been chosen for a reason; you have been chosen because you can make a difference in the career of a teacher, which ultimately means good things in the lives of our students.

MENTORSHIP MOMENT

LEARNING TO LOOK: THE FIELD TRIP DILEMMA

As I sat with Pat in the staff room, I could tell something was bothering him. The normally affable young man I had been working with since my principal had asked me to mentor him in late August was lost in thought. After a few minutes, when I was about halfway through my turkey sandwich, he finally began to talk. Apparently, a few of the students in his fifth-period science class had not handed in their permission form for the upcoming class field trip.

Pat was really excited for the students as they would be seeing the largest telescope in the region, which they had been studying in their astronomy unit. As I finished off my cookies, Pat was still grumbling that the students just did not understand how amazing this trip was going to be! Heck, he had even built in a stop at a local restaurant so they could get off the bus for a bit and break up the trip.

I had been helping Pat get organized for this trip. This included explaining how to book a bus, putting together a safety plan, and of course creating a permission slip with an itinerary that complied with district policy. Pat had made sure to prep the students and set up what he was convinced was going to be a great first field trip in his year of firsts. And what a year it had been! Even if we were only five weeks in, Pat had taken the school by storm with his energy and enthusiasm. Of course, there had been some bumps, and Pat had painted himself into a few corners. Totally normal for an emerging teacher.

As his mentor, when these bumps arose, I liked to ask him questions and let them sit for a bit. Thus, as I got up to head to my class, I asked, "What might the real problem be?" Pat quickly reacted, defending his field trip and asserting it was going to be "epic"! I smiled and suggested he look a bit further, just like the scientists do with the telescope he and the students were going to visit.

The next afternoon Pat popped into my classroom. He had figured out the problem. After our conversation he had taken a closer look at the situation and began to think deeply about the students and their reluctance to hand in their permission slips. He knew they were really interested in astronomy and had heard them talk about the trip when it was first announced. However, in reflection, he noticed their enthusiasm had dropped off a bit when he mentioned the restaurant stop.

I smiled as I knew the connections Pat was making but made sure not to get ahead of him or stifle his need to talk through the revelations he had made. He went on to say that he had talked with the Student Services teacher, and she had confirmed with him that some of the students were in situations where extra money for restaurants was definitely not in the family budget. She explained to him that instead of being embarrassed at the restaurant, unable to order, they would forgo the whole trip and use the permission slip now to avoid potential embarrassment later. I could hear the sadness in his voice as I knew he was making some big realizations about his students and the situations some of them face.

Once he finished talking, I gently asked what his plan was. Would it be full steam ahead or maybe a bit of a course correction? Pat held up the new permission slip. He had adjusted the itinerary, and instead of a restaurant the class would be stopping for a brown bag picnic, some fresh air, and a movement break at a roadside park he knew of. I smiled as he headed out to meet his class, knowing Pat was a little farther down the road toward his target of being the best teacher he could be and the teacher his students need—one who is willing to really look deeply at situations, find solutions, and help make schools a better place for all students.

The ABCDs of This Mentorship Moment

As you read through this Mentorship Moment, what were some biases that Pat may have exhibited in the situation? What were some of the attitudes and dispositions held by the mentor that helped Pat solve his problem?	
PAT:	**MENTOR:**

THIS INTERACTION BETWEEN MENTORING AND COACHING

Imagine you are at a staff meeting and a new teacher approaches you and asks you to explain the differences between mentoring and coaching. What would you say? How do you define these terms?

This is a topic that comes up a lot. In our many conversations about the "art and science" of being an effective mentor with an early career or new teacher, we felt it would be prudent to chat about the differences between mentoring and coaching. Both are important to developing the skills and capabilities in others, but these words are often used interchangeably when, in practice, they are different. Let's take a look at Table 1.1 and examine what we consider to be nuanced differences.

TABLE 1.1 MENTORING VS. COACHING

Domain	Mentoring	Coaching
Focus	***Developmental:*** Mentoring has a broader, long-term focus on overall personal and professional growth. It encompasses career development, personal development, and life balance.	***Goal-Oriented:*** Coaching is typically focused on specific goals, skills, or performance improvements. It is often used to address short-term objectives or particular challenges.
Scope	***Holistic:*** Mentors provide guidance and support across various aspects of the mentee's life and career, sharing their wisdom and experiences.	***Performance-Based:*** Coaches help individuals enhance their performance in specific areas, such as leadership skills, time management, or public speaking.
Relationship Dynamics	***Informal and Flexible:*** Mentoring relationships are generally more informal and flexible, adapting to the needs of the mentee over time. ***Personal Connection:*** Mentors often develop a deeper personal connection with their mentees, offering support and advice that can extend beyond professional concerns.	***Formal and Structured:*** The relationship between a coach and coachee is often formal and structured, with regular sessions, specific agendas, and measurable outcomes. ***Professional Boundaries:*** Coaches maintain a professional distance and do not typically get involved in the coachee's personal life beyond the scope of the coaching objectives.
Duration	***Long-Term:*** Mentoring relationships often last for a longer period, potentially spanning several years, as they focus on long-term development and career progression.	***Short-Term:*** Coaching engagements are usually shorter in duration, ranging from a few sessions to a few months, depending on the goals set.
Methods	***Advice and Sharing:*** Mentors provide advice, share their own experiences and insights, and offer guidance based on their personal and professional journeys. ***Role Modeling:*** Mentors serve as role models, exemplifying the attitudes and behaviors that can lead to success.	***Questioning and Feedback:*** Coaches use questioning techniques, active listening, and constructive feedback to help the coachee find their own solutions and strategies. ***Action Plans:*** Coaching often involves creating action plans, setting milestones, and tracking progress.

Domain	Mentoring	Coaching
Expertise	***Subject Matter Expertise:*** Mentors typically have significant experience and expertise in the mentee's field or industry, providing specific knowledge and insights.	***Process Expertise:*** Coaches may not need to be experts in the coachee's field but must be skilled in the coaching process and techniques.

Clearly, mentorship and coaching are deeply interconnected, yet they serve distinct, complementary roles in the development of new teachers. Coaching typically focuses on improving specific skills or practices through observation, feedback, and goal setting, helping teachers refine their teaching techniques in a structured, often short-term, way. While coaching is invaluable for honing classroom strategies and fostering professional growth, mentorship offers a broader, more holistic support system. Mentorship is about building relationships that nurture the personal and professional development of new teachers, guiding them through the challenges of their first years and providing a safe space for reflection and growth. Unlike coaching, which is often more performance oriented, mentorship is rooted in long-term support, emotional encouragement, and shared experience. It is through mentorship that new teachers can develop the confidence, resilience, and deeper understanding needed to thrive in the profession. Together, coaching and mentorship create a powerful framework for teacher development, but mentorship is the cornerstone for sustained success and fulfillment in the teaching profession.

While both coaching and mentoring aim to support individual growth and development, the big takeaway we ask you to bring forward with you in engaging with this book is that coaching is more performance and goal oriented with a short-term focus, whereas mentoring is developmental, long term, and relationship based. To help reinforce your understanding of this, we invite you to do the following exercise.

Exercise: Coaching or Mentoring?

All too often we interchange the words *mentoring* and *coaching*, believing them to be essentially the same thing. They are not. This exercise will assist you in understanding the distinctions between coaching and mentoring by applying the concepts to specific scenarios. See the end of the exercise for the answer key.

Instructions

Read through the following list of tasks and determine whether each task is related to coaching or mentoring. Write *C* for coaching or *M* for mentoring next to each task.

1. Providing guidance on navigating career advancement opportunities	
2. Setting specific, measurable, and time-bound goals for improving classroom management skills	
3. Sharing personal experiences about overcoming professional challenges	
4. Facilitating a series of structured sessions to enhance student assessment abilities	
5. Offering advice on work-life balance based on years of personal experience	
6. Developing an action plan to achieve a new skill within six months	
7. Listening and providing feedback on a mentee's long-term career aspirations	

8. Helping an individual identify and overcome limiting beliefs to boost confidence	
9. Introducing the mentee to valuable education stakeholders, partners, and networking opportunities	
10. Using questioning techniques to help a new teacher discover their own solutions to a problem	
11. Regularly meeting with a mentee to discuss their personal and professional growth over the years	
12. Creating a structured plan to improve time management skills within a new teacher	
13. Offering ongoing support and advice during significant career transitions	
14. Facilitating self-assessment exercises to improve specific teaching-related competencies	
15. Providing long-term support and advice based on a wealth of field experience	

Answer Key: Coaching or Mentoring?

1. Mentoring, 2. Coaching, 3. Mentoring, 4. Coaching, 5. Mentoring, 6. Coaching, 7. Mentoring, 8. Coaching, 9. Mentoring, 10. Coaching, 11. Mentoring, 12. Coaching, 13. Mentoring, 14. Coaching, 15. Mentoring

THE MENTOR AS A NAVIGATION (GPS) SYSTEM

When we introduced this chapter, we briefly mentioned the notion that the term *mentor* is often difficult to really define. In fact, for some of us, the word itself may draw up feelings of anxiety, discomfort, or even fear. The truth of the matter is, however, that the term is not nearly as important as the actions taken by you as a mentor. In a brief conversation between myself (Vince) and a dear colleague and friend, John Hattie (personal communication, January 26, 2024), we discussed the misinterpretations of mentorship and even his discomfort with the term itself. Ironically, when we were chatting, I was plugging in a destination on my maps program as we were driving in the middle of Alaska in the winter. At that moment I started to reflect on the commonalities between a mentor and a GPS.

Figure I.1: GPS

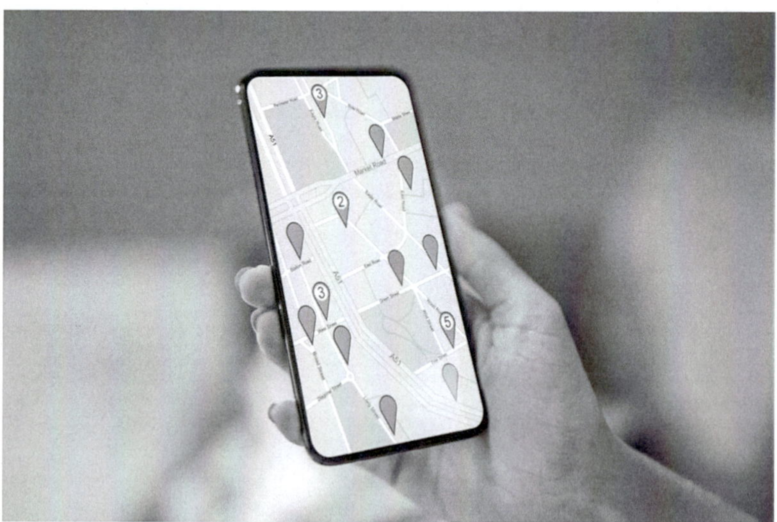

Source: istock.com/AndreyPopov

Hear us out. The actions of a GPS are not so different from what we do to support our mentees. A GPS knows the final destination of your journey, calculates the amount of time it will take to get to your destination, provides you with multiple routes, and perhaps most importantly adjusts all of these depending on the conditions or circumstances. You as a mentor have the potential to be a brilliant GPS for your mentee. You have been through those first few years of teaching, and have had experiences that your mentee may not have experienced. So, using your lived experiences and your expertise, you can help readjust the journeys of your new teachers, recommend alternative routes when necessary, determine whether they require collaboration (mentorship carpooling), and ultimately ensure your mentees are navigating through their first few years of teaching knowing you will be there looking out for them.

Not unlike a bad commute, sometimes the progress we make is slower than desired, but regardless, our GPS navigation and our mentorship is steadfast and always ensuring the journey is moving forward. It is with this mindset we are hoping you consider your importance as the navigation system for your mentee. So, now that you are equipped with the ABCDs of mentoring, we will set coordinates for our next waypoint (Chapter 2): helping you determine your mentorship modality (or default style of mentorship) through unpacking some *traditional*, *interdependent*, *metacognitive*, and *environmental* (T.I.M.E. methodologies) styles of mentorship.

REFLECTIVE PRACTICE

Through your understanding of the ABCDs, contemplate each of the following questions and consider your attitudes, biases, conceptual understanding, and dispositions as they relate to the prompts provided. Further, what are some new ideas gleaned in this chapter that you may want to try in addressing the provocations that follow? If you are mentoring someone for the first time, we invite you to approach these questions hypothetically: How would you do this? What might you say to your mentee?

1. In what ways do you help new teachers navigate the balance between following established educational practices and fostering their unique teaching style and creativity?
2. How do you foster a *growth mindset* in your mentees to encourage continuous learning and improvement in their teaching practices?
3. How do you address the diverse learning needs of new teachers and help them develop strategies to reach and engage all students in their classrooms?
4. How do you assist new teachers in developing strong connections and collaborations with colleagues, parents, and the broader school community to enhance the overall learning environment?
5. In what ways do you encourage new teachers to reflect on their teaching experiences, and how do you help them turn reflections into actionable insights for professional growth?

QUESTIONS TO ASK YOUR MENTEE (AND WHY)

Starting a new school year (or practice teaching session) with thoughtful and open-ended questions can help a mentor understand their protégé's needs, goals, and concerns. Here are five sample questions a mentor could ask their mentee:

1. **What challenges do you anticipate facing this year, and how can I support you in overcoming them?**
   Addressing potential challenges early on allows the mentor to offer guidance and resources. It also fosters a supportive environment, as the mentee feels comfortable discussing potential obstacles.

2. **What specific areas of professional development are you interested in exploring further?**
   Identifying areas of interest for professional growth helps the mentor tailor their guidance and support. It could involve recommending relevant workshops, courses, or resources that align with the protégé's interests and career goals. This also helps point to professional practice standards, which serve as a common language for growth and development.

3. **How do you plan to establish a positive classroom culture and build relationships with students?**
   Building a positive classroom environment is crucial for effective teaching. This question prompts the protégé to consider their approach to classroom management and relationship building, allowing the mentor to offer insights and advice.

UNPACKING OUR ABCDs OF MENTORSHIP MODALITY

In this chapter, we discussed the importance of understanding our *attitudes, biases, conceptual understanding,* and *dispositions* (ABCDs) toward mentorship. We offer two provocations for your reflection and consideration:

1. Having read this chapter on the ABCDs of mentorship, use the space provided to identify three ideas that have resonated most with you.

Idea 1.
Idea 2.
Idea 3.

2. With a colleague, share a mentorship motivation idea from this chapter that you will commit to trying with your mentee.

CHAPTER TWO

Determining Your Mentorship Modality

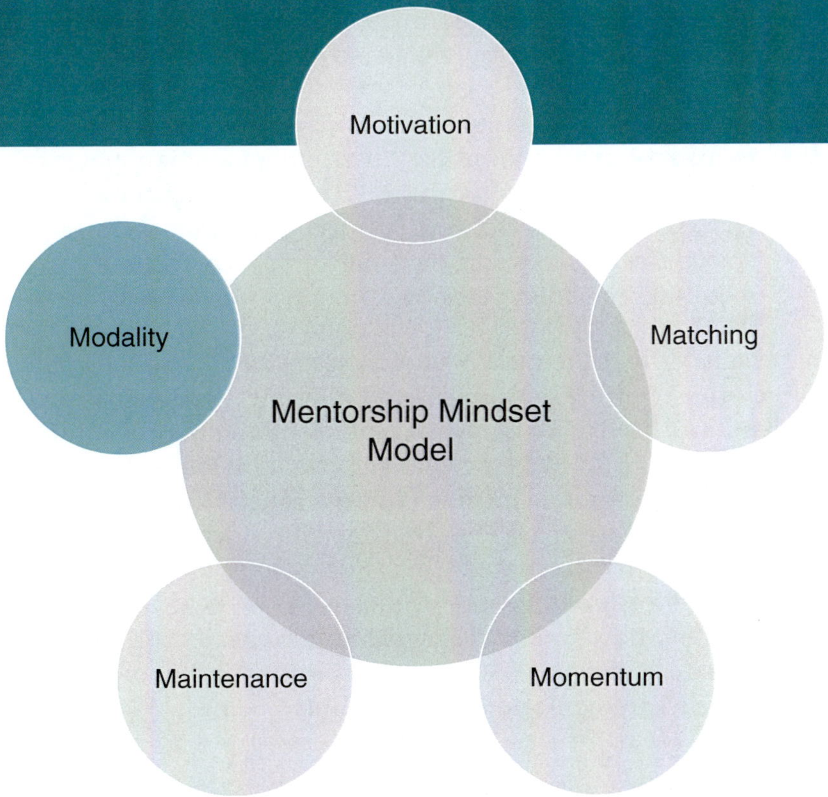

Motivation

Modality

Matching

Mentorship Mindset Model

Maintenance

Momentum

> A mentor is someone who allows you to see the hope inside yourself.
>
> — Oprah Winfrey (see McGivern, 2025)

Modality is one of those educational buzzwords that we like to use from time to time. In education, *modality* refers to the method or approach through which learning occurs or is delivered. It encompasses the various ways in which educational content is presented and interacted with. But what does it mean in terms of our practice as mentors? We invite you to think of your mentorship modality as how you bring your motivations about mentoring (your *why*) together with *how* you prefer to mentor another person. Let's explore this from a different angle.

In our technological world, we often hear the term *default setting*. This refers to the preconfigured option or value that a device, software, or system will automatically use if the user does not choose or change it. These settings are designed to provide a standard or optimal configuration for most users. For example:

- **In software:** A program might come with default settings for things like font size, theme color, or notification preferences. If you don't customize these settings, the software will use the defaults.
- **In hardware:** Devices like smartphones and computers have default settings for things like screen brightness, volume levels, and network connections. These settings ensure the device works right out of the box without requiring immediate user adjustment.

Default settings are usually chosen to be broadly suitable, but they can often be customized to better meet individual preferences or needs. We know that successful mentoring requires us to be mindful of better meeting the individual needs and learning styles of our mentee (a new teacher). What we invite you to do is to think about your modality (default setting) of how you prefer to mentor. Thus, this chapter on determining your mentorship modality is our way to help you better understand how your *attitudes*, *biases*, *conceptual understanding*, and *dispositions* (ABCDs) intersect with your approach or approaches to mentoring another human being.

MENTORSHIP MODALITY INVENTORY

In Chapter 1, we spent time asking you who you are as a mentor. We wanted to know your motivations in serving as a mentor. In thinking of your mentorship ABCDs, and in recalling those positive attributes of the people you deemed to be an effective mentor for you, we now invite you to complete the Mentorship Modality Inventory in Figure 2.1. Please ensure you answer to best reflect your positionality to the prompts.

Figure 2.1 ◆ Mentorship Modality Inventory

To what extent do you agree with each statement and its corresponding impact on creating effective mentorship? This inventory will provide you with a series of statements about mentoring. We invite you to read each statement and indicate the extent the statement resonates with you e.g. the extent to which you agree or disagree. Be sure to respond to allof the statements and answer based on your personal understanding and experience.

SCORING: 1 = totally disagree, 2 = somewhat disagree, 3 = neither agree / nor disagree, 4 = agree, 5 = totally agree.

Statement					
1. Mentorship is best viewed as a form of apprenticeship with the mentor serving as the experienced master.	1	2	3	4	5
2. Hands-on (practical) real-world experiences provide the most effective way to develop a mentee's skills.	1	2	3	4	5
3. Stimulating critical thinking skills through good questioning techniques is necessary for successful mentoring.	1	2	3	4	5
4. Developing trust is the most important aspect of successful mentorship.	1	2	3	4	5
5. To be effective, mentoring should take place over a longer period of time.	1	2	3	4	5
6. Good mentoring should see both the mentor and mentee learning from (and with) each other.	1	2	3	4	5
7. There needs to be opportunity for the mentee to teach or exchange knowledge with the mentor.	1	2	3	4	5
8. Ideally there should be a generational difference (gap) between mentor and mentee.	1	2	3	4	5
9. Mentoring should include knowledge sharing from multiple perspectives.	1	2	3	4	5
10. Regular feedback cycles focused on goal setting is a good way to foster continuous learning for a mentee.	1	2	3	4	5
11. The mentor and mentee should collaborate on setting realistic and attainable goals.	1	2	3	4	5
12. Mentors should teach the mentee specific cognitive strategies to promote problem solving, critical thinking and knowledge recall.	1	2	3	4	5

(Continued)

(Continued)

13. To be effective, any feedback must "feed-forward" to improve future learning outcomes.	1	2	3	4	5
14. It is important that ample time be given to focus on metacognition, problem-solving skills and the application of knowledge.	1	2	3	4	5
15. Mentorship must leverage self-inquiry, awareness of thought processes and self-directed learning.	1	2	3	4	5
16. Mentorship must include elements of cultural awareness, diversity and inclusion training.	1	2	3	4	5
17. Opportunities for mentor and mentee to engage in cross-cultural experiences are important for promoting deeper understanding of each other's backgrounds.	1	2	3	4	5
18. The sharing of cultural narratives (story-telling) is a key part of successful mentorship.	1	2	3	4	5
19. Human connection, creating a sense of belonging and breaking down stereotypes are essential to effective mentorship.	1	2	3	4	5
20. To be effective, mentoring pairings should seek like minded individuals with similar cultural backgrounds and beliefs.	1	2	3	4	5

Determining your preferred mentorship modality

- Add your scores for questions 1–5. These are considered **traditional** approaches to mentoring.
- Add your scores for questions 6–10. These are considered **interdependent** approaches to mentoring.
- Add your scores for questions 11–15. These are considered **metacognitive** approaches to mentoring.
- Add your scores for questions 16–20. These are considered **environmental** (learning culture) approaches to mentoring.

In the space provided, list your score for each of the four areas:

Mentorship Modality	Score
Traditional (Questions 1–5)	
Interdependent (Questions 6–10)	
Metacognitive (Questions 11–15)	
Environmental (Questions 16–20)	

Based on your responses, we will determine your "preferred" style (default setting) of mentorship and then dive into our T.I.M.E. approaches to mentorship. Recall that T.I.M.E. is our acronym for *traditional, interdependent, metacognitive,* and *environmental* approaches to mentorship.

PAUSE AND REFLECT 2.1

In noting your scores for each of the four areas, what stands out to you? Were there any surprises? What new questions might you have about your ABCDs of mentorship?

With a partner, discuss your results. If your partner knows you well, do they agree with your results?

POINTS OF CLARITY

Now that you have a richer sense of your ABCDs and preferred modality/approach to mentorship (T.I.M.E.), let's pause for a moment to shine some more light on these. It can be argued that many of the approaches to mentoring overlap and blend into each other. We would agree. For example, realistic goal setting (Question 11) could be considered a traditional approach in addition to a metacognitive one. We also want to be clear that *traditional* does not imply old or outdated. What is important here is the idea that the four areas should be viewed as complementary to each other versus stand-alone silos. We will each gravitate to the familiar and known approaches and likely use aspects from each of the four areas. Our challenge to you is to encourage you to consider using approaches in the areas within T.I.M.E. that are not your default, and consider how you might expand your modality (repertoire) of engaging with your mentee. So, if your highest score was in traditional approaches, for example, we invite you to try an approach from each of the other areas. Take a risk. Break out of your default style and try a new approach. Let's look at each of the T.I.M.E. approaches in detail. See Table 2.1.

TABLE 2.1 EXPLORING THE T.I.M.E. APPROACHES TO MENTORING

Traditional	Traditional mentorship methodologies vary across cultures and fields, but they often share common principles. These methodologies can be

(Continued)

(Continued)

	adapted and combined to suit the specific needs and cultural contexts of different individuals.
Interdependent	Interdependent mentorship methodologies emphasize mutual learning and collaboration between mentors and mentees. In these approaches, both parties contribute to each other's growth, fostering a relationship built on reciprocity.
Metacognitive	Metacognitive mentorship methodologies focus on developing mentees' awareness of their own thinking processes and strategies for learning. These methodologies encourage mentees to reflect on their learning experiences, set goals, and develop a deeper understanding of their cognitive processes.
Environmental	Effective environmental or cultural mentorship methodologies focus on creating a supportive and inclusive atmosphere where mentorship can thrive. These methodologies aim to address the unique aspects of the organizational culture or the environmental context in which mentorship takes place.

TRADITIONAL MENTORSHIP APPROACHES

The word *tradition* likely conjures as many (if not more) connotations as the word *mentor*. Yet, instead of understanding *traditional* as old or dated, we want you to think of it as *known or familiar practices*. These are perhaps the more tried-and-true approaches to mentorship that first come to mind. We often think of a master and apprentice construct like the guru on the mountaintop seeking to impart sage wisdom to the aspiring "grasshopper." While there are elements of this in traditional approaches, we recall that people are more likely to imitate the actions of models they perceive as similar to themselves (Bandura, 1989). We want to broaden the scope of what *traditional* means through inclusion of the power of story (narrative) and the sharing of cultural, generational, and classical approaches. These traditional mentorship approaches can be adapted and combined to suit the specific needs and cultural contexts of different individuals and organizations.

Traditional Mentorship Approach	Description	Characteristics
Community Elders or Wisdom Keepers	Found in many Indigenous cultures, where elders pass down knowledge, values, and traditions to younger members of the community.	a. Oral storytelling b. Experiential learning c. Cultural preservation
Long-Term Mentorship Relationships	Mentoring relationships that extend over a long period, allowing for continuous guidance and support.	a. Relationship building b. Trust development c. Ongoing feedback
Peer Mentoring	Mentoring that occurs between individuals at similar career or experience levels, with each person contributing to the other's growth.	a. Mutual learning b. Shared experiences c. Collaborative problem solving

Traditional Check-In: What do you think of the approaches, descriptions, and characteristics presented? Which ones do you use? Which ones do you want to try? Write your thoughts in the space provided.

INTERDEPENDENT MENTORSHIP APPROACHES

Perhaps the best way to understand *interdependent* is to think of the notion of learning "from and with" someone. This is also known as the reciprocity of learning. There is a reciprocal relationship where the mentor and mentee are open to learning together. It is a two-way street. Each party is open to learning something new from the other and is willing to be vulnerable, open, and honest about giving and receiving feedback.

The interdependent mentorship methodologies that we share here emphasize the importance of collaboration, shared responsibility, and ongoing learning between mentors and mentees. They contribute to a culture of reciprocity and continuous development within individuals and organizations.

Interdependent Mentorship Approach	Description	Characteristics
Actionable Feedback Loops	Regular feedback exchanges between mentors and mentees, with a focus on setting actionable goals and implementing changes based on feedback.	a. Continuous improvement b. Goal orientation c. Iterative learning
Cross-Generational Mentoring	Encourages mentoring relationships between individuals from different generations, fostering the exchange of insights and experiences.	a. Bridging generation gaps b. Knowledge transfer c. Reverse mentoring
Reciprocal Mentoring	A two-way mentoring relationship where both mentor and mentee take turns in sharing their expertise and learning from each other.	a. Role reversal b. Skill exchange c. Bidirectional feedback

Interdependent Check-In: What do you think of the approaches, descriptions, and characteristics presented? What ABCDs presented earlier in this chapter come to mind when you think of learning "from and with" your mentee? Write your thoughts in the space provided.

METACOGNITIVE MENTORSHIP APPROACHES

Thinking about our own thinking is one of the more powerful ways we learn. Bandura (1989) reminds us that through understanding our own cognitive and emotional dispositions and attitudes, we gain a sense of our self-efficacy. This means we possess a belief in our ability and capability to overcome challenges and navigate adversity. The stronger our self-efficacy is, the more likely we are to succeed and be resilient in the face of adversity. Lower self-efficacy, however, can lead to self-doubt and less favorable or negative outcomes. Thus, in understanding the power of cognitive coping strategies, impactful questioning techniques, and leveraging feedback to inform forward action, our mentees can come to realize higher levels of self-efficacy.

The metacognitive mentorship methodologies aim to empower mentees with the skills and awareness needed to take control of their own learning processes and continuously improve their cognitive abilities. The focus is on developing not only subject-specific knowledge but also the metacognitive skills that contribute to lifelong learning.

Metacognitive Mentorship Approach	Description	Characteristics
Feedback and Feedforward Sessions	Regularly providing feedback to mentees on their performance and helping them use this feedback to inform future actions. Mentors also guide mentees in setting goals for future improvement (feedforward).	a. Continuous improvement b. Self-reflection c. Goal-oriented learning
Goal Setting and Monitoring	Collaboratively setting short-term and long-term goals with mentees, and regularly assessing progress. Mentors provide guidance on setting realistic and achievable objectives.	a. Goal clarity b. Motivation c. Self-regulation

(Continued)

(Continued)

Metacognitive Mentorship Approach	Description	Characteristics
Metacognitive Questioning	Mentors encourage mentees to ask themselves metacognitive questions about their learning processes, such as "What strategies am I using?" or "What have I learned from this experience?"	a. Self-inquiry b. Awareness of thought processes c. Self-directed learning

Metacognitive Check-In: What do you think (speaking of metacognition) of the approaches, descriptions, and characteristics presented? Which ones do you think would have the greatest impact for you personally? Which ones do you want to try? Write your thoughts in the space provided.

ENVIRONMENTAL (OR CULTURAL) MENTORSHIP APPROACHES

We know that the learning environment is often referenced as the third teacher. We believe this to be profoundly true in mentoring. Creating an environment for mentorship is a key factor for the mentor to not only facilitate but implement. We think of a school's culture and how the staff can create the feel. Is it inviting and welcoming, or is it cold and sterile? Knowing we want to attract and retain teachers, it is incumbent to understand how to better create an environment for mentorship that stimulates unusual effort from apparently ordinary people. To do this we need to understand the strength found in cultural diversity, in school policy and procedures, and in our inclusive practices.

These approaches recognize the importance of cultural context and environmental factors in shaping effective mentorship experiences. By integrating cultural considerations into mentorship programs, organizations can create an inclusive and supportive atmosphere that benefits mentors and mentees from diverse backgrounds.

Environmental/Cultural Mentorship Approach	Description	Characteristics
Cultural Competency Training	Providing mentors and mentees with training on cultural awareness, diversity, and inclusion to enhance their ability to work effectively across different cultural backgrounds.	a. Cross-cultural understanding b. Sensitivity training c. Fostering inclusivity
Mentorship Circles or Affinity Groups	Forming mentorship circles or groups based on shared cultural or affinity traits, providing a supportive community for mentorship.	a. Group dynamics b. Shared experiences c. Community support
Storytelling and Cultural Narratives	Encouraging mentors and mentees to share personal stories and cultural narratives, fostering understanding and empathy.	a. Human connection b. Shared experiences c. Breaking down stereotypes

Environmental Check-In: What do you think of the approaches, descriptions, and characteristics presented? Describe the mentorship environment you seek to create. Write your thoughts in the space provided.

MULTIPLE APPROACHES TO MENTORSHIP

The T.I.M.E. approaches to mentorship are intended to provide an overview of the variety of different ways we can support new and early career teachers. In reality, though, there will most likely be opportunities to incorporate multiple approaches. This is especially true when you consider how certain people may respond to specific approaches. It is important to consider them all but not be compartmentalized into one category. Have a look at the following example from lifelong teacher and mentor Linda.

MENTORSHIP MOMENT

SUCCESSFUL MENTORING: BEING OPEN TO THE MOMENT

For 32 years, Linda had been a teacher at Middlehurst Elementary. While their school was located in an economically challenged part of the city, her students and their families prided themselves on their resiliency and toughness, though many of the more affluent residents of the community shied away from this part of town.

Since she began teaching, Linda had worked with a lot of new and early career teachers. As a new teacher, she received zero formal mentoring but was the recipient of much advice. Of course, not all the advice was good, but not all was bad either. One of the best pieces of advice was to be open to the moment. It would serve her well as she learned to adapt to all that a career in teaching could throw at her.

Somewhere along the way, she was asked to look after Riley, a young teacher who seemed to be struggling. She quickly discovered that while he was a bit of a genius with mathematics, his organizational skills were nonexistent. Linda, an English language arts teacher, could not help with the formulas but could see ways Riley could improve. So, she rolled up her sleeves and worked with him to put some structures in place that would allow his teaching to shine.

The next fall, Linda's school leader came knocking again. Alena was having trouble fitting in. By her own admission, the little teaching she had done was in a very small school with few students or resources. Linda worked with Alena to cocreate a plan to remedy this. Their regular meetings included looking at resources and introductions to members of the staff she could collaborate with. By the end of the year Alena was an integral member of the school team.

Over the coming years there would be others she would work with. Some were more straightforward while others might be described as outliers. One who would always remain close to her heart was Jacob Miller. He had grown up privileged, never encountering much in the way of "different." He had arrived at Linda's school in a bit of a huff after not getting any offers in the schools across town nearer to where he lived. Jacob had started the year by making statements to the students about the need for their parents to get involved, to volunteer, and to help fundraise.

The next morning, right after the parent group had left the principal's office, Linda was assigned to mentor Jacob. Linda began their first meeting by telling stories. These stories were about the community. She talked about the struggles and systemic racism. She talked about parents' desire for their children to succeed in the ways Jacob's parents had wanted him to succeed. But she also talked about their desire for their children to be proud of who they were and where they came from. She talked of being skilled in the ways of their grandparents, able to live off the land, to speak their traditional language. She referred to it as "two-eyed seeing."

Jacob sat stunned as the reality of his own blindness washed over him. He told Linda that as a little kid the few times he had ventured to the Middlehurst neighborhood he had seen things that just did not happen in his part of town. He had never gone back, and he'd grown up with images in his head that only now he was realizing were unfair and borne of bias. Linda had been clear that learning is important for everyone, and she was willing to lead if he was willing to follow.

In an article written about Linda when she retired, she was quoted as saying that being a mentor was an exercise in restraint. She explained that she believed, instead of forcing the mentee into a predetermined approach, she had been more successful "being open to the moment" with her mentees, allowing their needs and behaviors to guide her work. The author of that article—Principal Jacob Miller, the mentee who had never left—was living proof of her approach. He had been so struck by her mentorship he never even applied to leave. Her mentorship had changed his teaching, his outlook, and his life, putting the power of mentorship on full display.

Again, what we want you to carry forward, having read about the varied approaches Linda used in mentoring teachers over the years, is that the T.I.M.E. approaches we present are not meant to be viewed as silos. They are meant to serve as big ideas. In fact, we would even suggest that you consider them as mentorship playgrounds of sorts. The four "big idea" areas inherent to T.I.M.E. each present a suite of effective and proven approaches, but as witnessed through the work of Linda, there is not a one-size-fits-all approach. We encourage you to dabble in all of them. Do not be afraid to experiment and stretch your skills.

PRINCIPAL PERSPECTIVE ON MENTORING

To reinforce the importance of having a varied approach to mentorship, let's listen to the voice of a seasoned principal, Dr. Susan Coates, who has been involved in new teacher mentoring for many years in several K–12 schools. As you read her perspectives, be mindful of your experiences both as a new teacher being mentored and now in your role as a mentor. Consider the role your school leaders play or might play in supporting your growth and development as a mentor.

VOICE FROM THE FIELD

MODELING A COMMITMENT TO TEACHER MENTORING

Dr. Susan Coates, Principal, Austin O'Brien High School

With over 30 years of experience as a teacher, learning coach, assistant principal, and principal in diverse settings—rural and urban, K–12—I have come to deeply value the mentoring of new teachers. For me, this isn't just about induction and onboarding; it's about fostering a nurturing culture that supports teacher growth, competency, and retention. I believe that every new teacher—whether they're practicum students, early career educators, international teachers new to Canada, or individuals transitioning from other professions—deserves to feel welcomed, valued, and supported as they join our school community.

Mentoring is crucial to the success of our school environment. Yet, I've seen firsthand that often the process of connecting new teachers with mentors can be haphazard. In both small remote areas and larger urban centers, finding a willing mentor can sometimes feel like a game of chance rather than a carefully thought-out pairing. This needs to change. New teachers are a vital investment in our educational community, and our approach to mentoring should reflect the importance of this investment.

In my career, I've encountered situations where teachers, who I wouldn't have chosen as mentors, ended up in these roles, sometimes using the time more for their own prep rather than fully engaging with their mentee. I firmly believe that principals must be actively involved in selecting mentors to ensure that the motivation and dedication required for effective mentoring are present. I make it a priority to have meaningful conversations with my teachers about the importance of mentoring, asking questions like "What is your style or approach to mentoring?"

Mentorship should not be a reflection of how we ourselves were mentored. It's crucial for principals to be directly involved in the mentoring process to demonstrate its significance. By actively participating, I can model the commitment to developing our new teachers, which encourages the same attitude throughout the entire staff.

Investing in professional development to enhance mentoring skills is essential. We need to explore best practices and understand our own attitudes and preferences toward mentoring. This focus is not just about attracting new teachers but also about designing supportive structures that make them feel like integral and valued members of our learning community.

When we thoughtfully support seasoned teachers in their mentorship roles and equip them with effective training, everyone benefits—the new teachers, the mentors, the entire profession, and, most importantly, the students and families we serve. It's about creating a thriving community where every member has the opportunity to grow and succeed.

We know that school leaders are critical to the success of teacher mentorship. When school leadership is invested in mentorship development, there is greater commitment from teachers to step into the role of mentor. As you continue to learn about approaches to mentoring in this chapter, we invite you to have conversations with your school leaders in terms of what you feel would be helpful for your growth and development as a mentor.

PAUSE AND REFLECT 2.2

Having read the views of Dr. Coates, what aspects of mentorship motivation (Chapter 1) and mentorship modality stand out for you? What are two key takeaways from her thoughts on mentoring new teachers?

T.I.M.E. for a Check-Up

Read the following sequence of mentoring actions that depicts how Mrs. Sampson, a Grade 5 generalist with 15 years of teaching experience in K–6, works with Alex, who is a student teacher, on his final field experiences practicum (a nine-week experience). With a successful practicum, Alex will become certified as a new teacher.

For each of the eight actions used by Mrs. Sampson, focus on the bold portion of text. What connections to the T.I.M.E. approaches do you see in place? Specifically, indicate if you believe each action is a traditional, interdependent, metacognitive, or environmental approach. We have done the first one for you as an example. We will also provide a key that shares our suggested responses.

Observation and Reflection

1. **Observation:** Mrs. Sampson starts by allowing Alex to observe her classes for the first week. During this period, **Alex watches how Mrs. Sampson manages the classroom, engages with students, and implements lesson plans**. He takes notes on her teaching style, student interactions, and classroom management techniques.

T.I.M.E. Connections:

*This is primarily a **traditional approach** of watching a more experienced other demonstrating expected (or exemplary) practice. It is not dissimilar to a master and apprentice approach.*

2. **Reflection and Discussion:** After a week of observation, Mrs. Sampson schedules a meeting with Alex. They discuss what Alex observed, focusing on effective teaching strategies, student engagement, and any challenges. **Mrs. Sampson encourages Alex to reflect on what worked well and what could be improved.**

T.I.M.E. Connections:

Modeling and Guided Practice

3. **Modeling Lessons:** In the second week, Mrs. Sampson invites Alex to **coteach** a lesson. Mrs. Sampson models the lesson while Alex assists, giving Alex the opportunity to see how to implement the teaching strategies in practice. **They plan the lesson together, discussing the objectives and the methods to be used.**

T.I.M.E. Connections:

4. **Gradual Responsibility:** As the weeks progress, Mrs. Sampson gradually hands over more responsibility to Alex. Alex starts leading parts of the lesson while Mrs. Sampson observes and offers feedback. **This approach helps Alex build**

confidence and develop his teaching style under the guidance of an experienced mentor.

T.I.M.E. Connections:

Feedback and Support

5. **Constructive Feedback:** After each lesson or teaching segment led by Alex, **Mrs. Sampson provides specific, constructive feedback**. For example, she might highlight how Alex's use of questioning techniques effectively engaged students but also suggest ways to improve classroom management or clarity in instructions.

T.I.M.E. Connections:

6. **Encouraging Professional Growth:** Mrs. Sampson **encourages Alex to set personal goals for improvement** and to seek out additional resources, such as teaching workshops or educational literature. She also helps Alex reflect on his progress and celebrates his successes to build confidence.

T.I.M.E. Connections:

One-to-One Mentorship

7. **Regular Check-Ins:** Mrs. Sampson schedules regular one-to-one meetings with Alex to discuss his experiences, address any concerns, and provide additional guidance. **These check-ins offer Alex a safe space to ask questions and seek advice** on any challenges he's facing.

T.I.M.E. Connections:

8. **Providing Resources:** Mrs. Sampson shares educational resources, lesson plan ideas, and classroom management strategies with Alex. **She also introduces Alex to professional networks or groups where he can connect with other educators.**

T.I.M.E. Connections:

Additional Questions About Mrs. Sampson's Mentorship Modality

a. How would you describe Mrs. Sampson's overall mentorship modality?

____
____
____
____
____

b. With a colleague, discuss what other approaches might be helpful in supporting Alex.

____
____
____
____
____

Answer Key

1. Traditional; 2. Metacognitive (reflective practice); 3. Interdependent (coplanning); 4. Environmental (trust, confidence building); 5. Metacognitive (feedback); 6. Metacognitive (goal setting); 7. Environmental (safe check-ins); 8. Environmental (supportive community).

a. Although there are aspects of traditional and interdependent aspects at first, Mrs. Sampson appears to espouse more environmental and metacognitive stances within her mentorship modality.

IMPROVING OUR MENTORSHIP IMPACT

As we conclude this chapter on mentorship modality, consider the following three reflective questions and considerations of how your professional identity as both a teacher and a mentor intertwine:

1. **How do my own teaching philosophies and experiences influence the advice and feedback I give, and how might this impact the new teacher's development?**
   - Reflecting on this question helps mentors assess whether their personal biases or teaching styles are overshadowing the needs and perspectives of the new teacher. It encourages them to consider if their guidance is adaptable to different teaching (mentoring) approaches and whether it's genuinely supportive of the new teacher's growth.
2. **In what ways can I better model effective teaching practices and problem-solving strategies during my interactions with the new teacher?**
   - This question prompts mentors to evaluate how well they demonstrate the behaviors and skills they are advocating. By modeling effective practices and addressing challenges constructively, mentors can provide practical examples for the new teacher to follow.
3. **How can I balance offering guidance with empowering the new teacher to develop their own teaching style?**
   - This question encourages reflection on the mentor's approach to providing support. It's important to offer constructive feedback and share experience while allowing the new teacher the space to explore their own methods and philosophies. Finding this balance can help foster both growth and independence.

Use this space to note any further wonderings or key learning points that you take away from this chapter.

CONCLUSION

In Chapter 1, we invited you to think about your mentorship motivations. In essence we wanted you to think about your *why* in wanting (or having) to serve as a mentor. We did this through the ABCDs of mentoring. In this chapter we wanted you to gain awareness of your preferred approach or style (modality) of mentorship. The T.I.M.E. approaches to mentorship helped to do this. In the next chapter, we are going to spend some time with one of the most critical, yet often least considered, aspects of mentoring: mentorship matching.

UNPACKING OUR ABCDs OF MENTORSHIP MODALITY

In Chapter 1, we discussed the importance of understanding our attitudes, biases, conceptual understanding, and dispositions (ABCDs) toward mentorship. We offer two provocations for your reflection and consideration:

1. Having read this chapter on mentorship modality, what are your ABCDs toward the need to be more attuned to how you like to mentor? Use the space provided to identify three ideas that have resonated most with you.

Idea 1.
Idea 2.
Idea 3.

2. With a colleague, share a mentorship modality idea from this chapter that you will commit to trying with your mentee.

CHAPTER THREE

Creating an Environment Fit for Teacher Mentorship

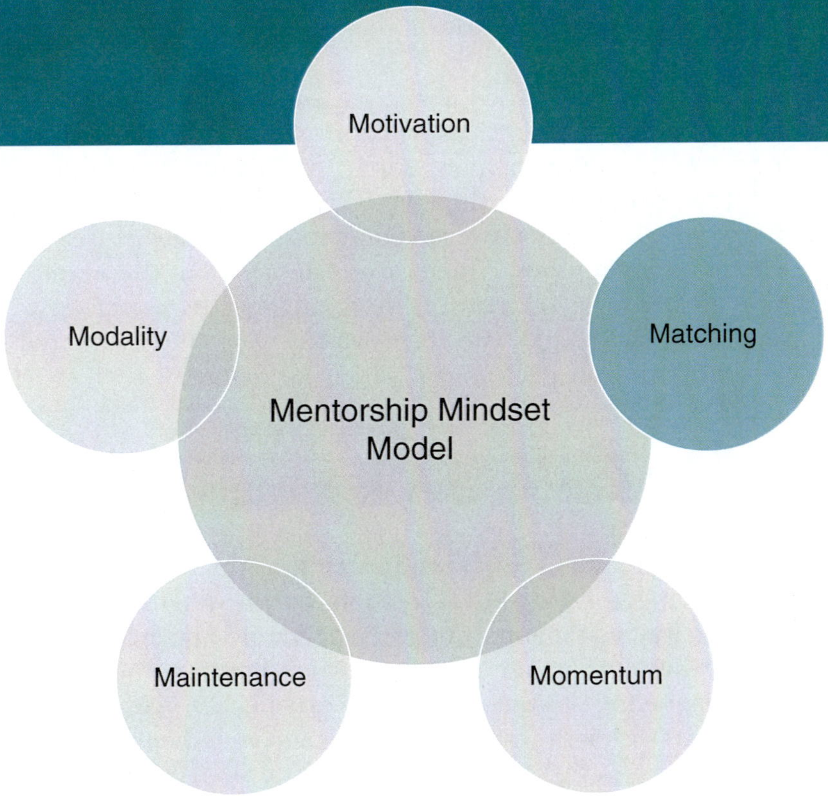

Motivation

Modality

Matching

Mentorship Mindset Model

Maintenance

Momentum

I've learned that people will forget what you said, people will forget what you did, but people will never forget how you made them feel.

— Maya Angelou (see quoteresearch, 2014)

YOU ARE A TEACHER MENTORING ANOTHER TEACHER

We often hear the word *fit* in conversations about mentorship. "Is the person I am mentoring the right fit for me?" and vice versa are common wonderings and questions we hear from both the mentor and the mentee. We can think of fit as meaning suitable or appropriate. We often refer to fit as a form of matchmaking. Remember that old expression "a match made in heaven"? We know that the nature of the mentorship pairing can make or break the relationship and heavily impact the chances of success. While we firmly acknowledge that, sometimes, "we get who we get so don't be upset," we advocate for a greater level of intentionality and discernment on the part of practical placement planners, principals, and system leaders in charge of determining who will mentor whom.

In Chapter 1, we learned about our mentorship motivations through *attitudes*, *biases*, *conceptual understanding*, and *dispositions*, or the ABCDs of mentoring. In Chapter 2, we gained insights on our mentorship modality and explored how we mentor. In this chapter, we are going to spend time focused on who we are mentoring. Thus, we will speak about the need to have greater focus on mentorship fit and discuss several environmental factors that can help you to create conditions that will enhance your relationship with your mentee.

SENSING THE ENVIRONMENT

This chapter proposes to have you gaze into a mirror so you can act upon the mentorship ABCDs you hold, as this will in turn influence the way you mentor others. Furthermore, the chapter will explore the role that the environment you establish as the mentor has in garnering positive mentorship experiences, "creating the conditions" for both you as the mentor and your mentee(s).

SEEING THE "WHO BEFORE WE DO"

We are big fans of seeing the "who before we do." This means that, as a mentor teacher, you need to invest the time, effort, and energy in getting to know your mentee before you press into the growth and learning ahead. You need to get to know them, not just as a new teacher, but in a holistic sense of who they are. You will also need to reflect on who you are to them. This is not always comfortable to do. Mentorship pairings can sometimes feel contrived or forced with no initial spark of connection. We will talk about how to achieve this and give you solid strategies to put into practice so that you can make more meaningful and intentional connections to your mentee.

In our discussions with teachers across Canada and the United States, what we noticed most was that the mentorship of early career teachers (ECTs) was inconsistent at best. Mentor teachers (you) might not have received much (if any) training in how to serve as an effective mentor. Far too often, mentorship is left to chance. We want to bring more design to mentor teacher preparation and will steady the ladder for you to climb and reach new heights as an effective teacher mentor.

As a mentor teacher, you may engage with university staff who coordinate and support placements of student teachers. Often there are university field staff who also visit your classroom when you are working with your mentee. Typically, they provide additional eyes and ears to support you in working with your mentee. You will most certainly interact with your school leadership about the ECT you are supporting. Whereas this book is purposed to help you deepen your mentorship skills, it is important to have perspectives of the placement dynamics of those very preliminary student teacher matches in addition to the new teachers (including second career) whom you will be supporting. We will explore perspectives of an experienced mentor teacher who now serves as a placement coordinator. That will be followed by some perspectives of how school administration can support you.

VOICES FROM THE FIELD

A CONNECTIONS-BASED APPROACH TO MENTOR-MENTEE MATCHING

Chantel Lussier Napier, MEd

Northwestern Polytechnic (Grande Prairie, Alberta, Canada)

In my role as educational coordinator, responsible for beginning teacher practicum placements, I imagine the big-picture view of an educational ecosystem. I see a vast and complex network where schools, leaders, teachers, and communities eagerly await protégés who desire a guided entry into the system. In preparation for tackling hundreds of mentor matches in an academic year, acknowledging the complexities of education environments by first examining the full scope affords a holistic view to ready us for matching.

This practice always reveals logistical factors. We often encounter variables such as new locations or changes in leadership. At times, we realize that what's needed are more teachers with open minds to open doors. Or perhaps we realize that there are plenty of willing and capable teachers, yet they are new to mentorship and in need of enhanced guidance through the role.

A well-designed navigation system for both mentors and mentees ensures sustainability. Maintaining smooth processes to suit your needs is foundational work that cannot be overlooked. It retains satisfied mentors guided by clear expectations and support, securing ample placement options to ease the matching process. It also maximizes the likelihood of positive experiences that foster professional identity in early career teachers, with lasting benefits beyond the timeline of practica or internship. Not only do we want to set them up for a strong start; we want to set them up for longevity in the field.

It is crucial for system leaders to support this work by understanding mentorship impact. Defining the role of a mentor and articulating a shared vision for a successful mentorship experience ensures collaborative involvement of all partners. This proves helpful when school principals put forward their best mentor candidates and take an active role in recruitment; thanking a veteran for volunteering yet again or tapping someone on the shoulder who would not consider mentoring without a vote of confidence makes the difference between being equipped with a strong pool of mentors and not being so equipped.

The notion of matching has a connotation of sameness, so it often results in putting together people with similar grade levels, subject areas, or positions. Perhaps we need to focus less on finding a matching pair and more on creating a unique partnership.

A connection-based lens is helpful to ponder what we know and appreciate about individuals, to see their potential as partners, and to connect the dots across the network. It's then that we can intentionally cultivate a connection that promises success. When planning a match, consider this: Can they complement one another as copartners/comrades/collaborators?

The benefit of small networks is that you are more likely to "know your people," which is helpful for matching. Yet it can be tricky to coordinate placements in rural or remote areas with options limited by small schools, fewer mentors, multigrade classrooms, location barriers, and time constraints as staff divvy extras such as administration and coaching. Conversely, in networks with many individuals, relationship-based considerations become challenging to apply if you do not know individuals well. Learning about your mentors/mentees can be achieved through curated questionnaires to build a profile. Rather than being paired by similar teaching assignments, matches should be made by considering what each person brings to the partnership.

Each carries unique strengths and lived experiences, so expecting them to be more different than the same not only recognizes but values each person's offerings. After all, a mentorship match is reciprocal and should mutually benefit both. From my vantage point, a mentor teacher preparing for a new mentorship match should spend time considering the following:

- What do I hope to learn from this individual?
- What leadership competencies do I hope to strengthen through my service as a mentor?
- What skills/strengths might my mentee bring to the partnership?

The best matches are those that grow the mentor as much as the mentee.

SCHOOL LEADER PERSPECTIVE ON MENTORSHIP MATCHING

It was the lessons learned in my first two principalships that fueled my passion to want to be a better mentor and champion for teachers. I (Tim) recall the array of feelings I held when I was appointed principal of a large Grade 7–12 school. Having just served as principal of a small inner-city elementary school, I went from leading a staff of 8 (140 students) to one of 80 (1,100 students). At first, it seemed daunting and overwhelming. Then I realized that, in many ways, it was more challenging to meet the needs of a smaller school community given that the teachers had to wear multiple hats versus having the ability to spread out the workload over many people at the larger site. Regardless of the size of the school and the number of staff, developing others meant that I needed to continue to develop my own capability to serve as an effective mentor. Beyond that, helping the teachers I served to become more empowered and intentional in their mentorship was an ongoing goal.

As principal, I learned that it is essential to be vested in the work of your mentor teachers. Do not take it for granted that they have all the support and resources needed to be successful. I have experienced the extremes of a laissez-faire (hands-off) approach as well as a micromanagement (too hands-on) approach from my leaders when I was working with ECTs.

What was constant at both schools was my desire to help steady the ladder for each staff member. What do I mean by "steady the ladder"? It is a concept I acquired as a junior naval officer. Steadying a ladder while a teammate climbed offered them stability and safety, which ultimately contributed to mission success. The ladder is also a metaphor for climbing to success—reaching potential. It means that as a leader, as a mentor, I need to get out of the way and let each person climb to their own next best step. The last thing I ever wanted to be was the leader who gazed down upon the team and said, "You should see the view from up here." Being a mentor includes providing ways to uplift someone else to new heights. It is being a contributor (helper) to the success of someone else.

For me, this would be achieved in part through creating an environment that would help me realize greater leadership capacity from my team. *Creating the conditions*, a phrase I first heard in 2015 at a conference where Sir Ken Robinson was speaking (TED, 2015), inspired me to truly understand and appreciate the power of establishing a school culture (environment) where not only students, but also teachers and staff, could flourish. It became a focal point for me. "At the most fundamental level, the focus of education has to be on creating the conditions in which students will want and be able to learn. Everything else has to be arranged on that basis"

(Robinson & Aronica, 2015, p. 72). If creating the conditions is what is best for students, then it should also be the case for adult students—especially our mentees.

The desire I espoused to create a school culture steeped in a growth mindset and predicated in collegial trust and respect eventually enticed me to pursue doctoral studies in understanding the self-efficacy of aspiring leaders. Teachers, whether new, early career, or having years of experience, are leaders. Let's unpack this statement a bit more. Within the classroom teachers lead a learning community, are instructional leaders, and leverage resources and materials in support of teaching and learning. Designing a mentoring program that helps all teachers see themselves as leaders of learning is what we are truly seeking in the writing of this book.

In this chapter, we are going to explore topics that are central to creating an environment for effective mentorship to take root and flourish. Among these topics are *trust* and *respect*—two terms that can be generally misconstrued when applied together in the context of mentorship. It is important to understand that, although trust and respect play an interdependent role, they are individually significant to the impact that a mentor can have on a new or beginning teacher. We have intentionally chosen to discuss this topic here because the matching of mentors and mentees must be carefully considered, intentional in design, and never left to chance.

THE IMPORTANCE OF TRUST AND RESPECT IN MENTORSHIP MATCHING

Trust. This word carries a lot of weight. In everyday life we consciously and unconsciously engage in matters of trust. For example, when a headline appears on your newsfeed, do you willingly accept it as truthful, or are there elements of doubt? Do you believe the words of colleagues and friends—even family—at face value? These are examples of how we consciously consider what we believe to be true versus false.

Do you trust that your Uber driver or airline pilot will get you to your destination safely or that your drive-thru order is going to accurately reflect what you ordered? These fall into the realm of unconscious trust, a blind trust that everyday type of things will happen as they should. Truth has become relativistic—that is, there may be many interpretations of truth. Increasingly, we observe that facts blur with opinion, critical thinking subsides to feelings, and, as a society, our default setting is more likely switched to mistrust. In our book *Leader Ready: Four Pathways to Prepare Aspiring School Leaders* (Cusack & Bustamante, 2023), we spend a good amount of time talking about the critically important role that trust plays in fostering effective relationships. We firmly believe that "effective mentorship and leadership development cannot occur without trust" (Cusack & Bustamante, 2023, p. 68).

What, then, are the key areas within mentorship that trust impacts? Here are six that we believe should be top of mind when creating the conditions for trust with your mentee:

1. **Open Communication:** Trust fosters an environment where new teachers feel safe to openly discuss their challenges, uncertainties, and questions without fear of judgment. This allows mentors to provide effective guidance and support tailored to the mentee's needs.
2. **Effective Feedback:** Trust enables mentors to give constructive feedback that is well received and acted upon by the mentee. When there is trust, feedback is seen as a tool for growth rather than criticism.
3. **Risk-Taking and Innovation:** In a trusting mentor–mentee relationship, new teachers are more likely to take risks in their teaching practices and experiment with innovative methods. They feel supported in trying new approaches, knowing that their mentor has their best interests at heart.
4. **Emotional Support:** Teaching can be emotionally challenging, especially for new teachers. Trust allows mentors to provide emotional support, helping mentees navigate the ups and downs of their early teaching experiences.
5. **Professional Growth:** Trusting relationships facilitate ongoing professional growth. Mentors can introduce new teachers to professional networks, resources, and opportunities for continuing education, confident that their mentee will value and utilize these opportunities.
6. **Retention and Job Satisfaction:** New teachers who feel supported and trusted are more likely to stay in the profession and feel satisfied with their career choice. This can contribute to higher retention rates and a more positive overall experience in the teaching profession.

In essence, trust forms the foundation of a mentoring relationship, enabling effective communication, growth, support, and, ultimately, the success of new teachers as they navigate their early career stages. This must encompass perspectives of different generations in the workforce today, cultures, and ways of learning. Wayne reminds us of the following: In considering the context of many Indigenous cultures, we can see the importance of elders and senior members of family groupings such as uncles and aunties working alongside (and not simply directing) less experienced members of their families and communities in learning the roles they will eventually fulfill. When spending many months (and in some cases years) working alongside each other in the transmission of culture and ways of knowing, seeing, and doing, the ability to be vulnerable enough to take risks has to be grounded in trusting relationships.

TRUST IS THE CORNERSTONE OF EARNING RESPECT

Why do we place such a high value on the development of a mentoring environment that is both trustful and trust filled? The simple answer is the level of growth or success of the learning of the mentee will be limited if there is not a measure of trust in the mentorship being offered. As the cornerstone of an effective mentorship pairing, trust is the foundation upon which respect is built. You have most likely heard the adage: "You can trust someone but not respect them, and respect someone but not trust them." The worst case in a mentorship relationship is when there is low trust and low respect. What we want for you is to offer insights and practical ways to move toward the ideal model, which is *high trust* and a *high level of respect*. This is the sweet spot where mentoring will flourish and be most impactful. Take a look at Figure 3.1 to better see how the intersection of trust and respect factors into the mentoring environment you are seeking to create. Our goal with this is to reinforce the centrality that trust and respect have in fostering effective mentorship relationships (dynamics) so that they may take root, blossom, and flourish. Our hope is to give you as a mentor of an ECT more insights in how to achieve trusting and respectful outcomes.

Figure 3.1 • Trust vs. Respect

Trust	Respect
In the context of teacher mentorship, *trust* refers to a mutual confidence in the reliability, integrity, and abilities of both the mentor and the mentee. 1. ***Reliability:*** Trust involves the expectation that both the mentor and the mentee will consistently fulfill their commitments, such as meeting regularly, adhering to agreed-upon plans, and following through on promises. 2. ***Integrity:*** Trust requires both parties to act with honesty and ethical behavior. This includes being truthful in communications, maintaining confidentiality about sensitive discussions, and upholding professional standards. 3. ***Competence:*** Trust is built on the belief that the mentor has the necessary knowledge, skills, and experience to provide valuable guidance, and that the mentee is capable and willing to learn, grow, and apply the insights gained from the mentorship. We can think of this as mentor credibility. 4. ***Support and Encouragement:*** Trust involves a commitment to support and encourage one another. The mentor should provide guidance and constructive feedback while fostering a safe and positive environment where the mentee feels confident to express challenges and seek advice. 5. ***Open Communication:*** Effective mentorship relies on open, transparent, and respectful communication. Both parties should feel comfortable sharing their thoughts, asking questions, and providing and receiving feedback without fear of judgment. 6. ***Empathy and Understanding:*** Trust includes showing empathy and understanding toward each other's experiences, challenges, and perspectives. This helps in creating a supportive and collaborative mentoring relationship. 7. ***Consistency and Dependability:*** Trust is reinforced through consistent and dependable behavior. Regular and predictable interactions help build a sense of stability and reliability within the mentorship.	In the context of teacher mentorship, *respect* refers to a mutual regard for each other's roles, experiences, and contributions within the relationship. 1. ***Valuing Expertise:*** Respect involves recognizing and appreciating the knowledge, skills, and experience that both the mentor and the mentee bring to the relationship. This includes acknowledging the mentor's expertise and the mentee's potential and perspectives. 2. ***Professional Courtesy:*** Both parties should demonstrate professional courtesy in their interactions. This includes punctuality, preparedness, and attentiveness during meetings, as well as maintaining a polite and considerate tone in communication. 3. ***Acknowledging Individuality:*** Respecting each other's individuality means understanding and valuing differences in teaching styles, backgrounds, and approaches. It involves creating an inclusive environment where diverse perspectives are welcomed. 4. ***Constructive Feedback:*** Providing and receiving feedback in a constructive manner is a vital aspect of respect. This means offering feedback that is honest yet supportive and receiving feedback with an open mind and a willingness to improve. 5. ***Confidentiality:*** Respect includes maintaining confidentiality about the discussions and challenges shared within the mentorship. This fosters a safe space for open and honest dialogue. 6. ***Empathy and Understanding:*** Demonstrating empathy by being attuned to each other's challenges and successes helps build a supportive and respectful relationship. Understanding and addressing concerns or difficulties with compassion is essential. 7. ***Encouragement and Support:*** Respect is also shown through encouragement and support, helping to build confidence and motivation. Celebrating successes and providing encouragement during challenges are important aspects of a respectful mentorship.

Now that we have considered how inextricably trust and respect are connected, we want to spend some time on the importance of why you, as a mentor teacher, need to strive to instill high levels of both trust and respect in your mentee. This visual, presented in Figure 3.2, is intended to help in understanding how the dynamics of trust and respect can impact the effectiveness and quality of mentoring relationships for new teachers. When it comes to mentoring new teachers (especially in the hopes of retaining them in the profession), we must strive to achieve high levels of both.

Figure 3.2 ◆ The Intersection of Trust and Respect

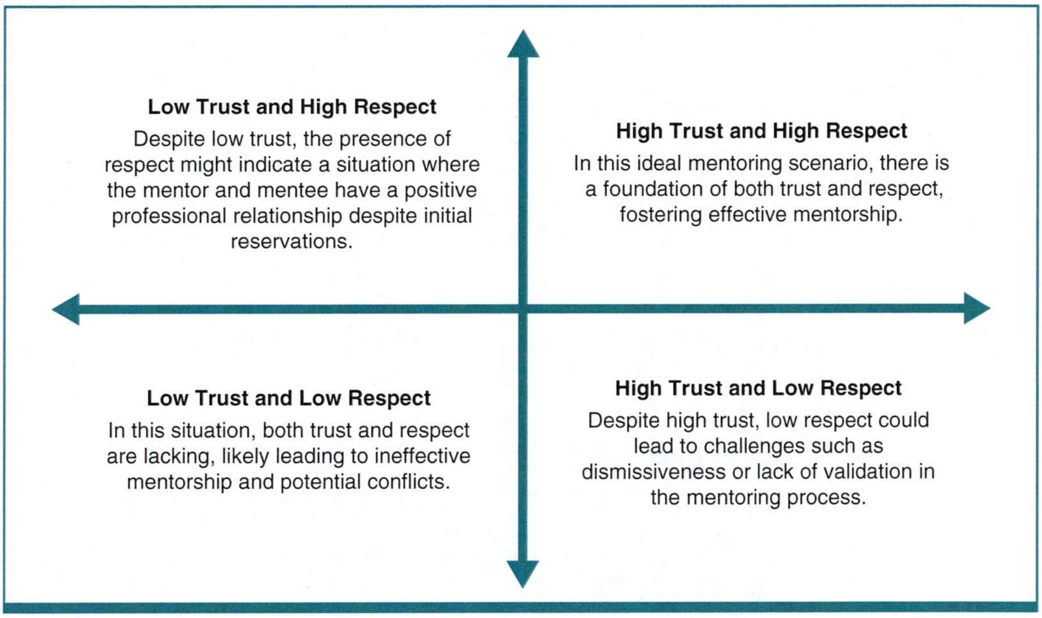

Low Trust and High Respect
Despite low trust, the presence of respect might indicate a situation where the mentor and mentee have a positive professional relationship despite initial reservations.

High Trust and High Respect
In this ideal mentoring scenario, there is a foundation of both trust and respect, fostering effective mentorship.

Low Trust and Low Respect
In this situation, both trust and respect are lacking, likely leading to ineffective mentorship and potential conflicts.

High Trust and Low Respect
Despite high trust, low respect could lead to challenges such as dismissiveness or lack of validation in the mentoring process.

High levels of trust and respect in new teacher mentorship can significantly enhance the mentoring process in several key ways:

1. **Open Communication and Feedback:** When there is trust and respect between mentors and new teachers, it creates a safe environment where open communication can flourish. New teachers feel comfortable seeking guidance, asking questions, and sharing concerns. Mentors, on the other hand, are more likely to provide constructive feedback in a supportive manner, knowing that it will be received positively and used for professional growth.
2. **Effective Collaboration and Support:** Trust and respect foster a collaborative relationship where both mentor and new teacher can work together effectively. Mentors can provide targeted support tailored to the needs

and goals of the new teacher, offering resources, strategies, and insights that are valuable and relevant. This collaborative (interdependent) approach allows for mutual learning and development, benefiting both parties.

3. **Increased Confidence and Professional Growth:** When new teachers feel trusted and respected by their mentors, it boosts their confidence in their abilities. They are more likely to take risks, try new teaching strategies, and reflect on their practice openly. This environment of trust and respect nurtures a growth mindset, encouraging continuous professional development and improvement.

Overall, high levels of trust and respect create a positive mentoring relationship that is essential for the success and well-being of new teachers as they navigate their early career challenges and opportunities. Furthermore, as mentors we must come to understand that regardless of our title or credentials, respect should be *earned and never demanded*. Focusing on creating an environment steeped in trust is the best way to earn the respect of those whom you mentor. This allows us to better see the "who before we do." Next, we will build on this some more in exploring the skill, will, and thrill of our mentee.

THE ROLE OF SKILL, WILL, AND THRILL TO CREATE OPPORTUNITIES FOR HIGH TRUST AND HIGH RESPECT

Trust in teacher mentorship manifests when our ECTs see that their mentor truly believes in them—especially when they struggle. As effective mentors, we must have the expectation that ECTs will be successful, and that we will help guide them to success.

Trust in teacher mentorship manifests when our early career teachers see that their mentor truly believes in them—especially when they struggle. As effective mentors, we must have the expectation that early career teachers will be successful, and that we will help guide them to success. Part of our expectation of new teacher success is predicated on how much we know about the skill, will, and thrill of our new teachers. Taking time to determine what capacities they come to us with will help strengthen our relationship with our early career teachers as well as creating a more trusting bond.

KNOW THE SKILL, WILL, AND THRILL OF YOUR MENTEE

Each individual brings with them a unique set of knowledge, skills, and attitudes. Not unlike the dispositions our students have, our new teachers have unique capabilities that may be unnoticed if we do not get to know our people. As a mentor, you should *actively* engage in getting to know new teachers both professionally and personally. While we realize you cannot force a personal relationship, we believe there are always ways to bring about a collegial rapport that gives you sufficient insight about the individual. This helps us build on the strengths and interests we learn of and allows us to make more well-considered decisions; we can anticipate the impact of our decisions when we know the *who* behind the person prior to engaging in the *what* of mentorship.

We can anticipate the impact of our decisions when we know the *who* behind the person prior to engaging in the *what* of mentorship.

In our work in schools, we have discovered it's beneficial for mentors to lean on three main attributes in getting to know their mentees in order to more precisely tailor mentorship experiences. Hattie and Donoghue (2016) inspired the idea of the skill, will, and thrill of student learning. This was modified in 2023 when Cusack and Bustamante used the same attributes to recognize talent in aspiring school leaders. We feel the inclusion and modification of this process to recognize what our new teachers/mentees bring with them is a critical aspect of the mentorship matching process. Figure 3.3 describes what we mean when we discuss the skill, will, and thrill of new teachers.

Figure 3.3 ◆ The Skill, Will, and Thrill of New Teachers

Skill	Refers to what prior knowledge the new teacher brings with them. This can be previous teaching experiences, knowledge of local teaching standards, and understanding of teaching. These are what our new teachers bring with them as they enter the doors of their classroom.
Will	Refers to the new teacher and their disposition toward teaching. The specific dispositions will determine how a teacher may respond when confronted with new or challenging classroom or school situations.
Thrill	Refers to the teacher's motivations. Essentially, this includes their passion toward their "students" learning and development, and their desires to engage in teaching to their best possible ability.

Let us unpack how we might use specific questions to better determine the skill, will, and thrill of new teachers as we engage in the mentorship matching process.

QUESTIONS TO ASK YOUR MENTEE

SKILL

- How do you plan and structure your lessons to ensure that all students, regardless of their learning abilities, can access the content?
- How do you assess student learning and progress? What methods do you use to provide feedback that supports growth?
- What strategies will you use to ensure that all students are engaged and learning, especially those who may struggle or excel in different areas?

WILL

- What do you believe makes an effective teacher, and how do you see yourself working toward that?

- How do you plan to handle the challenges of your first year in teaching?
- How do you plan to continue learning and growing as a teacher throughout your career?

THRILL

- How do you plan to build relationships with your students and create a positive classroom environment?
- What do you hope to achieve in your first year of teaching, both for your students and for your own professional growth?
- As a new teacher, how might you celebrate successes, in terms of both your students' learning and your own teaching journey?

Taken together, skill, will, and thrill comprise a person's sense of self-efficacy. By understanding the skill, will, and thrill of our new teachers, we can design the environment in which they can flourish. This will help solidify the impact we can have by taking time to engage in the process of knowing what prior experiences our new teachers have had. For now, we recommend taking a few minutes to pause and ponder with the following reflection question.

By understanding the skill, will, and thrill of our new teachers, we can design the environment in which they can flourish.

PAUSE AND REFLECT 3.1

Based on the definitions of skill, will, and thrill explained in this chapter, what strategies might you implement to gain a better understanding of where your new teachers are in their development?

MENTORSHIP MOMENT

HELP IS DOWN THE HALL

It was midafternoon on a warm spring day at Mountain View Elementary School, and the usually lively classroom of Ms. Parker was in a state of chaotic disarray. Pencils flew like javelins across the room, voices bubbled over one another, and the whiteboard was adorned with an impromptu mural of doodles. Ms. Parker, a young and passionate teacher in her first year, stood at the front with a mixture of frustration and helplessness on her face.

After the bell rang for recess, Ms. Parker sighed deeply and made her way down the hallway to Mrs. Thompson's classroom. Mrs. Thompson, a veteran teacher known for her calm demeanor and effective classroom management, was someone Ms. Parker deeply respected and admired.

Knocking softly on the door, Ms. Parker entered to find Mrs. Thompson arranging some books on a shelf. "Oh, hello, Ms. Parker," Mrs. Thompson greeted her warmly. "What brings you by?"

"Mrs. Thompson," Ms. Parker began hesitantly, "I'm really struggling with classroom management. My students seem to have endless energy, and I can't seem to get them to settle down and focus."

Mrs. Thompson nodded knowingly, gesturing for Ms. Parker to take a seat. "It can be tough in the beginning," she empathized. Recalling similar challenges in her first year as a teacher, she inquired, "Tell me, what strategies have you tried so far?"

Ms. Parker explained her attempts at using a class reward system and implementing a seating chart, but how neither seemed to have a lasting impact. "I feel like I'm constantly redirecting behavior and not actually teaching," she confessed, frustration evident in her voice.

Mrs. Thompson listened attentively, then offered a gentle smile. "Building a positive classroom environment takes time and consistency," she advised. "Have you tried setting clear learning intentions from the beginning of each lesson? And reinforcing positive behavior with specific praise?"

Ms. Parker nodded, taking mental notes. "I've tried, but maybe I need to be more consistent with it."

Mrs. Thompson nodded in agreement. "Consistency is key. Why don't we plan to observe each other's class in the next couple of days and then discuss some approaches to how to encourage higher levels of student engagement? After all, teaching is a team effort."

Feeling a weight lifted off her shoulders, Ms. Parker thanked Mrs. Thompson sincerely. "I really appreciate your advice. I'll keep working at it and look forward to visiting your class and having you visit mine."

As Ms. Parker left Mrs. Thompson's classroom, she felt renewed determination. She knew that building effective classroom management skills would take time, but with the guidance of mentors like Mrs. Thompson, she was confident she would get there.

PAUSE AND REFLECT 3.2

1. What advice would you have offered to Ms. Parker on how to address her problem of practice?
2. What do you think about the approach Mrs. Thompson used to help Ms. Parker? In your view, what worked well? What might you do differently?

BUILDING COMMUNITY IN MENTOR–MENTEE RELATIONSHIPS

As a school leader, each August, I (Wayne) looked at my staff list. Interspersed with the names of all the returning staff were the new hires along with a few student teachers. I knew that handing them off to random members of staff who were designated as "mentors" was not a guarantee that things would go well. Not only was I concerned with who would be a good mentor for each particular new hire or student teacher in terms of skill development, but I also had to think about how relationships could be built in relatively short order. The school year rolls at a frenetic pace, and before you know it, opening day has been replaced by Thanksgiving Day celebrations. However, before you can talk about how to build community, you must understand how relationship building, as outlined by Peck (1998), works.

The first is what is referred to in the literature as the building of pseudocommunity or pseudorelationships. Many of us are familiar with the superficial "making nice" we all do when we encounter new people, whether it is following a move to a new school or at the start-of-the-year staff meeting with the new people who have just joined. Everyone wants to make a good impression, and thus the conversation is kept to the mundane. We ask each other questions about the weather and how our summer was. We do our best to avoid potentially controversial issues such as politics, religion, or going too deep into questions of family.

The next phase begins to bring honesty as a search for commonness in position creeps in. Quiet questions about what the point of the icebreaker was, predictions about whether the newly announced district strategies will make it to the winter break or not, and such are bandied about. This somewhat negative talk serves a purpose as people attempt to get a sense of each other's positions and whether or not they can work together.

As time wears on, some people (if not all) will begin to "empty" or share important thoughts and facts that will allow people to begin to truly see them. This is the most important stage. It is when vulnerability comes to the fore. It allows people who might not have appreciated each other's viewpoints to gain a deeper understanding of each other and in many cases gain empathy. Finding out that you and your colleagues are all nervous about the midterm exams or discovering that a cantankerous colleague has a loved one battling cancer will undoubtedly bring greater understanding and may allow you to become closer. If people cannot pass through this stage, it is unlikely they will reach true community. Think back over your career and who you "bonded" with. We would hazard a guess it might not have always been over a mutual love of how quadratic equations are taught. Instead, it might have been because you found ways to be vulnerable and empathetic toward each other. This stage can take time and is unlikely to happen overnight.

Once the emptying stage has completed itself, the final stage of true community can be entered, and the work of mentorship can truly begin. The mentor and the mentee are beginning to understand and accept each other, strengths, flaws, and all. It is when we can become vulnerable with each other that true growth for both mentor and mentee can begin to occur.

When many of us think back to the mentors or mentees we most enjoyed working with, we recognize this process has occurred. We were open and honest with each other, warts and all. No, we are not advocating a complete baring of souls and secrets, but we are saying that to get to a place where mentors and mentees genuinely care about each other, you will need to get past the superficial and move deeper.

ENVIRONMENT MATTERS

By actively assisting in building a community, mentors and school leaders create an environment where new teachers can share ideas, resources, and best practices. This environment of collaboration encourages continuous learning and innovation, helping new teachers to develop effective teaching strategies and improve their instructional skills with the support of their mentors, allowing their more experienced colleagues to actively and meaningfully contribute to their development. Mentors and school leaders who come together provide a network of support, where new teachers can express their challenges and frustrations. This support system helps reduce feelings of isolation and burnout, contributing to the mental well-being of new educators. However, it is important that these moments do not devolve into gripe sessions about students, systems, or other challenges and instead are moments of celebration or creativity in the examination of potential or actual solutions.

A strong community helps new teachers build confidence in their abilities. Positive relationships with experienced mentors and supportive school leaders reinforce a sense of belonging and validation. If we think back to the earlier concept of elders and older members of Indigenous communities taking on less experienced members of the community, we can think about how we are interrelated with members of our own worlds who stepped up to help us "learn the ropes" in a way that never made us feel less than or incompetent, but rather left us feeling empowered and ready to keep trying. This support is crucial for teacher retention, as feeling part of a cohesive community can increase job satisfaction and commitment to the profession. Developing the attitudes that no challenge is too big and that problems are simply another opportunity to learn contributes to collective efficacy, a powerful force enabling a school to be a tremendous place for students to learn.

Importantly, this feeling that comes from a community that is able to successfully meet challenges will drive the community's ability to attract and retain its membership. Teachers, like most other people, enjoy being part of successful operations, and a school that is doing well and has a strong sense of community acts much like a magnet or strong gravitational pull, keeping members over the long term and thus allowing them to become even stronger.

Building a strong sense of community between more experienced teachers and those who are emerging is crucial for fostering a collaborative and supportive educational environment. Here are a few effective ideas that mentors, in conjunction with school leaders, can implement:

- **Group Mentorship Programs:** Establish formal mentorship programs where teachers of varying and similar levels of experience are grouped together. This provides structured opportunities for experienced teachers to share their wisdom and support new teachers in navigating the school culture, curriculum, and classroom management as well as allow for opportunities for teachers new to the profession to work together to work out mutual challenges without immediately being given the answer by a more experienced mentor and short-circuiting their learning.
- **Collaborative Professional Development:** Organize professional development sessions that encourage mixed groups of veteran and new teachers to collaborate on projects and share best practices. This fosters mutual respect and learning, allowing both groups to benefit from each other's experiences and fresh perspectives. Another decision that has to be made is who goes to opportunities that involve experiences outside of the school such as conferences. Some schools are clear that the veterans have earned the right to travel while junior members of staff can wait their turn. This can send a strong message to staff and create needless challenges. As has been spoken about earlier, opportunities for making more personal social connections are important, and

taking two or three days to travel, learn, and spend time together can have a dramatic impact on staff cohesion once back at the school.

- **Shared Goals and Projects:** Encourage veteran and new teachers to work together on schoolwide initiatives, such as curriculum development committees or extracurricular programs. Shared goals and collaborative projects can unite teachers in their efforts to improve the school community and student outcomes. It will also increase the likelihood of seeing the hidden talents that each of us possesses.

RELATIONSHIPS MATTER

If you want to go fast, go alone. If you want to go far, go together.

— African proverb (see Goldberg, 2016)

Every successful project I (Wayne) have witnessed in education has been the result of a group of staff, students, and caregivers in some sort of combination that worked toward a common goal. A quick scan of cultures across the world would seem to support that thought, at least from a historical perspective. I would offer barn raisings, the harvest, and the buffalo hunt as such examples. It would seem, then, that when the whole (or at least a significant part of the school community) comes together, they achieve more than they could have alone as individuals.

Many of those endeavors were difficult and at times quite stressful. However, for some reason these individuals stayed together, persevered, and succeeded. No doubt there were moments when things were bleak, ready to fracture and fall apart. So why didn't they? If you looked closely at the moments when things were verging on collapse, the glue that usually held things together were the relationships. Maybe you were down going into the last inning, or the set was not ready the night before the opening show, yet you still found a way to triumph. No doubt relationships had been built, at least to some degree, in the time leading up to the work that made leaving harder than staying. It is like this in many organizations and groups—people had come to trust and believe in each other's abilities and knew that what they said they would do they would do.

Relationships between mentors and mentees are similar. They are the foundation of effective mentorship, playing an important role in personal and professional development. They take time and are built over time through moments when trust, communication, and mutual respect is tested and ultimately proven, thereby creating an environment conducive to learning and growth.

Relationships provide a sense of connection and support for both mentors and mentees. As a mentor, you will offer guidance and encouragement, helping the mentee navigate challenges and setbacks with confidence. In return, mentees bring fresh perspectives and enthusiasm, revitalizing mentors' passion for their work. Sometimes the mentee can develop a sense of efficacy when they have usable advice for you that they see you use successfully. Many of our newer colleagues have much to say on leveraging technology, new ideas, and ways of seeing the challenges we have faced and perhaps not been able to move the needle on to our satisfaction.

As such, it is important to remember that relationships are a two-way street where trust and respect must flow both ways. A mentor shares their expertise and experiences, empowering mentees to develop new skills and competencies without making the mentee feel they are a "lucky recipient." Nor do they just give their answer each time—instead coming alongside the mentee to help them reflect and figure out what the best answer is for them. A good mentor is clear that this process is cherished as a way to ensure that our collective mission as educators will continue.

Furthermore, relationships encourage accountability and commitment. Mentors hold mentees accountable for their goals and actions, creating opportunities for authentic "wins" and providing a chance to reflect on and discuss what worked and, of course, what did not. In turn, mentees demonstrate dedication and perseverance, striving to meet and exceed expectations set by their mentors.

Ultimately, relationships between mentors and mentees create a supportive ecosystem where both parties thrive. By investing in these relationships, mentors and mentees lay the foundation for lifelong learning and success. Thus, relationships truly matter in mentorship, serving as the catalyst for personal and professional growth.

THE IMPORTANCE OF RELATIONSHIPS IN INDIGENOUS MENTORSHIP

Examining the value of relationships between mentors and mentees in many cultures, especially those that are Indigenous, we quickly see that "living in relationship" with each other is very important as a base construct in how people work together. This concept is rooted in the traditions and values of many Indigenous communities as evidenced by how elders pass knowledge to younger generations, how the community interacts with the environment, and, even historically, how Indigenous people interrelated with the settlers and visitors who never left, acting in good faith and reciprocity. In many Indigenous cultures, mentorship is not limited to professional or educational exchanges but is a holistic practice that encompasses all aspects of life, as evidenced through the following:

- **Cultural Continuity:** Mentorship in Indigenous communities often serves as a way to pass down knowledge, traditions, and language. Elders and mentors pass down wisdom and practices that are crucial for the cultural survival and continuity of the community. This process fosters a sense of identity and belonging in mentees, grounding them in their heritage.
- **Community and Collective Responsibility:** Indigenous worldviews as reflected in the Circle of Courage (four key growth needs essential to human well-being: Belonging, Mastery, Independence, and Generosity) and Te Ao Māori (the worldview of the Māori people of Aotearoa, or New Zealand) emphasize interconnectedness and collective well-being. A mentor–mentee relationship is seen as part of the larger picture with the building and maintenance of relationships that sustain the community. Mentors guide mentees not just for individual success or status but to benefit the entire community, instilling values of collective responsibility. In the case of educators, this might be best phrased as "What are we doing for the students, and how will it benefit them as our next community leaders?"
- **Holistic Development:** Unlike Western concepts of compartmentalization, Indigenous mentorship approaches recognize the mentee as a whole person, addressing spiritual, emotional, physical, and intellectual growth. This holistic approach ensures that the mentoring relationship

nurtures all aspects of the mentee's life, fostering balanced development and resilience. As we hear more teachers talk about life–work balance, this concept of wholeness becomes more and more relevant to mentors who were forced to "run with the herd" immediately and handed many extra duties as part of their onboarding.

- **Working and Learning Alongside Each Other:** Indigenous mentorship practices see the mentor and mentee learning and growing together. This mutual respect and shared learning reinforces the bonds between generations and contributes to the strength and cohesion of the community. For any experienced teacher who was humbled by the sudden need to quickly and successfully adapt to a digital and remote teaching environment at the onset of the pandemic, it became clear what many of our younger colleagues could teach us.

From an Indigenous perspective, the importance of relationships in mentorship goes beyond the more experienced teacher handing down their wisdom to a mentee who happily receives and employs those lessons. Instead, Indigenous mentorship talks about living in relationship with each other, respectfully sharing knowledge, and allowing the mentee the time and space to employ some or all of the ideas.

FOSTERING A SENSE OF BELONGING

Source: istock.com/Janet Griffin-Scott

Every fall on the prairies, I watch thousands of geese gathering and training in their V formations to prepare for the long journey south. I'm sure you have read the stories about how geese change who is at the front and continually honk as a way to encourage each other on their arduous trip south. We know that flying in the V formation actually makes the work easier for the geese, another example of the benefits of traveling together rather than alone. It is clear they belong to each other as a group and there are mutual and individual benefits experienced.

Belonging is the cornerstone of meaningful relationships, profoundly impacting the way individuals connect and form bonds with others in schools. Its importance has existed since time immemorial for many cultures and groups around the world. Brendtro and colleagues (2019) have written about belonging in their work on the Circle of Courage. The Māori hold the concepts of *whakapapa* ("genealogical connections") and *whanaungatanga* ("family relationships") sacred as part of Te Ao Māori, and the Kodiak Alutiiq people talk about *Suupet*—a responsibility to each other and themselves. When people feel a sense of belonging, whether it's within a family, a community, or a workplace, they are more inclined to open up, trust others, and engage in authentic interactions.

Belonging fosters empathy and understanding, allowing individuals to recognize and appreciate the perspectives and experiences of others. When people feel accepted and valued for who they are, they are more likely to extend the same acceptance and respect to others, thus creating a supportive environment for building strong and lasting working relationships.

As this is the same for the mentor–mentee relationship, how, as the mentor, do you foster a sense of belonging for your mentee not just with you but in the larger organization? Whether they are a student teacher, a new hire who is also new to the profession, or an experienced veteran joining your school team, they will be innately searching for some sense of belonging. Each, dependent on their personalities and lived experiences, will need to feel belonging to a different level. Some will want to be an embedded part of the team, wearing all the school pride gear they can get their hands on, while others might be a bit more standoffish and perhaps just enjoy some lunchroom banter but decline the weekly invitation to the staff gathering.

The important part is that an offer is made in a variety of formats. I know of one school leader new to a building who spent many of his free moments in the band room talking to the music teachers about jazz and all things musical in his quest for belonging.

Thus, as a mentor, it is important to make the first move, to find ways to foster your mentee's sense of belonging whether that be through a school T-shirt or going for a cup of coffee after school. Many teachers have found their belonging through extracurriculars or by being encouraged to share some time and space with colleagues. Whatever you decide to do, remember they may be apprehensive and may need a few different opportunities to begin developing a sense of belonging with you and the school in general.

CONCLUSION

So now that we have talked about your motivations and modality to mentorship as well as the process of matching, we will now move to Part II of the book where our focus shifts to the practical experiences of mentorship. Before we go, though, let's check in on your mentorship ABCDs.

UNPACKING OUR ABCDs OF MENTORSHIP MATCHING

In Chapter 1, we discussed the importance of unpacking our *attitudes*, *biases*, *conceptual understanding*, and *dispositions* (ABCDs) toward mentorship. We offer two provocations for your reflection and consideration:

1. Having read this chapter on mentorship matching, what are your ABCDs toward the need to be more intentional and deliberate in mentorship pairings? Use the space provided to identify three ideas that have resonated most with you.

Idea 1.
Idea 2.
Idea 3.

2. With a colleague, share a mentorship matching idea from this chapter that you will commit to trying with your mentee.

CHAPTER FOUR

Building Mentorship Momentum

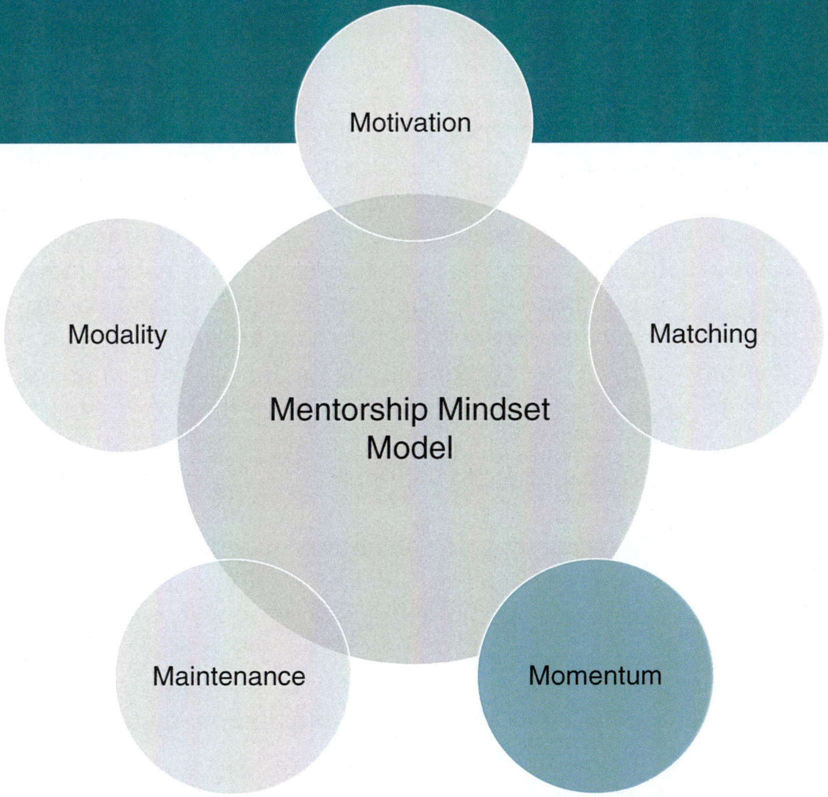

Motivation

Modality

Matching

Mentorship Mindset Model

Maintenance

Momentum

> One of the greatest values of mentors is the ability to see ahead what others cannot see and to help them navigate a course to their destination.
>
> — John C. Maxwell (2015, p. 212)

BUILDING MENTORSHIP MOMENTUM

Do you remember learning about the differences between potential and kinetic energy in science class? Potential energy is the energy an object possesses due to its position, condition, or state. It is "stored" energy that has the potential to do work. Chapters 1 through 3 in this book have helped us build the potential for success in our mentorship motivations, modality, and matching. We have learned our ABCDs (*attitudes*, *biases*, *conceptual understanding*, and *dispositions*) of mentoring, explored our approaches to mentoring via T.I.M.E. (*traditional*, *interdependent*, *metacognitive*, and *environmental* approaches), and deepened our understanding of why greater intentionality in mentorship matching is value added. In essence, the first half of this book has raised the level of our mentorship potential. We have raised our mentorship mindfulness to new heights.

Kinetic energy is the energy an object possesses due to its motion. Any moving object has kinetic energy, which depends on its mass and speed. The faster an object moves and the more mass it has, the more kinetic energy it possesses. For example, a rolling ball and a moving roller coaster both have kinetic energy. For us, mentorship momentum refers to the continuous, progressive energy and focus in a mentoring relationship that propels both the mentor and the mentee toward achieving their goals. It is the sustained progress in learning, growth, and development, driven by consistent engagement, constructive feedback, and goal-oriented actions.

In the next two chapters, we will become kinetic by unleashing your mentorship potential through momentum-building practices that put that potential energy to work. We will explore routines, structures, supports, and processes that move you and your mentee forward. First, let's consider the following metaphor that links our understanding of building momentum.

METAPHOR: THE MENTORING JOURNEY AS A ROLLER-COASTER RIDE

Potential Energy: The Starting Point

Imagine a new teacher at the top of a roller coaster, filled with excitement, ideas, and untapped skills—their *potential energy*.

This is the starting point of their career, representing the knowledge, enthusiasm, and fresh perspective they bring. Just like a coaster car perched at the highest peak, the teacher's potential energy is vast but not yet in motion.

Kinetic Energy: The First Drops and Twists

As the roller coaster starts to move, potential energy converts into *kinetic energy*—the teacher begins applying what they've learned, trying out lessons, engaging with students, and navigating the twists and turns of the classroom. This energy is the active engagement, the learning on the fly, and the practical experience that transforms theory into practice. The ups and downs represent the challenges and successes that keep the ride dynamic.

Momentum: Building Confidence and Consistency

With each loop and turn, the coaster gains *momentum*—just as the teacher gains experience, confidence, and consistency in their practice. This momentum makes it easier to tackle new challenges because the teacher isn't starting from scratch anymore; they're moving forward with the combined force of their past experiences and learned skills. As momentum builds, the ride becomes smoother, and the teacher is better equipped to handle the ups and downs with skill and resilience.

Mentorship: The Tracks That Guide the Ride

The mentorship provided (by you) serves as the track, guiding the new teacher's journey. Without a well-constructed track, the ride could be chaotic, but with proper guidance, the teacher's energy—both potential and kinetic—channels into productive and meaningful directions, building momentum toward becoming a skilled and impactful educator. Our goal for this chapter is to help you build momentum with your mentee. So press play on your favorite "walk-up" song, set up at the plate, and get ready to hit a home run as we throw some great mentorship momentum–building ideas your way.

ANDRAGOGY VS. PEDAGOGY

One of the first big steps in laying the tracks to build mentorship momentum is to think about how you, as an adult, prefer to learn. In this instance, we are wanting you to think metacognitively about how you prefer to learn as an adult. Let's be honest; when it comes to our own professional development (PD), there are activities we definitely prefer over others. If hearing "crisscross applesauce" by a facilitator at a staff PD session to get your attention has you thinking "I'd rather have a root canal than be here," then what you need is a facilitator who understands andragogy. That's right—adults learn differently from how we teach children. *Andragogy* refers to the methods and practices of teaching adult learners. The term emphasizes the unique needs and characteristics of adults in the learning process. Simply stated, adults do not want to be taught the same way in which students are taught (*pedagogy*). Thus, having a sense of how to engage your mentee as an adult learner, even though you are ultimately helping them to be great with all things pedagogically, is what your mentee wants. Like you, they are an adult learner and thus need to be treated and mentored as such. In Table 4.1, we share five key ways of how andragogy differs from pedagogy.

TABLE 4.1 KEY DIFFERENCES BETWEEN ANDRAGOGY AND PEDAGOGY

Andragogy	Pedagogy
Self-directed Work with the new teacher to set individualized professional goals that align with their strengths and areas of improvement. Use these goals as a basis for their learning plan. Goal setting helps shift the focus from mentor-led guidance to self-driven progress, fostering independence. Personalized goals give mentees ownership of their learning journey and make the mentoring process relevant and meaningful to their specific needs.	**Dependent on the teacher** Pedagogy often places the teacher at the center of the learning process, with students positioned as passive recipients of knowledge. The teacher delivers information, and students are expected to absorb it. This model conditions students to rely on the teacher (in this case you as mentor) for guidance, answers, and validation, limiting their ability to think independently or explore topics on their own.

Andragogy	Pedagogy
Practical application and problem solving Present mentees with real classroom challenges or case studies and guide them in finding solutions through research, discussion, and experimentation. Encourage them to analyze the problem, propose solutions, and reflect on the outcomes. Instead of giving direct answers, guide them to brainstorm solutions, weigh options, and test different strategies.	**Content delivery** Traditional pedagogy often emphasizes rote learning, memorization, and the recall of information rather than encouraging students to engage in deeper, exploratory, or inquiry-based learning. This approach teaches students to rely on the teacher for facts and correct answers instead of fostering a mindset of exploration, questioning, or independent problem solving.
Learner-centered Encourage new teachers to undertake small independent projects, such as researching a teaching strategy, implementing it in their classroom, and sharing the outcomes with you as mentor or other peer groupings. Independent projects give new teachers the chance to take ownership of their learning and build self-efficacy.	**Teacher-centered** Feedback in pedagogical approaches is typically given by the teacher, often focusing on right or wrong answers rather than encouraging students to self-reflect or seek alternative solutions. This creates a cycle of dependency, where students look to the teacher for validation and corrections instead of learning to assess and improve their work on their own.
Intrinsic motivation (self-improvement) Encourage new teachers to keep a reflective journal where they can document their experiences, challenges, and successes. Facilitate reflective discussions where they can analyze their teaching practices. Reflection helps new teachers think critically about their actions and develop their own insights, reducing reliance on external validation.	**External rewards (grades, praise)** Pedagogy often rewards compliance and following instructions over creativity or initiative. The focus is on completing assigned tasks rather than exploring personal interests or finding unique solutions. This can dampen students' willingness to take risks or make decisions without the teacher's approval, fostering a dependent learning attitude.

Andragogy	Pedagogy
Flexible learning, experience-based Begin with modeling (I do, you watch), then move to guided practice (We do together), and finally reach independent practice (You do, I observe). Provide feedback along the way but gradually reduce the level of direct intervention. Experiential learning reinforces practical skills and helps new teachers learn from real-world classroom experiences, making theory come alive.	**Structured, curriculum-based** Pedagogical models often follow a set sequence of instruction, where each step is defined by the teacher, leaving little room for deviation or independent exploration. This predictability can limit students' ability to navigate uncertain or open-ended tasks, making them reliant on the teacher for the next steps.

PAUSE AND REFLECT

How do the principles of andragogy shared in Table 4.1 inform or influence your ABCDs of mentorship? What is one key takeaway that you will focus on in working with your mentee?

Mentoring new teachers using andragogical approaches focuses on principles of adult learning that encourage self-direction, practical application, and reflective practice. The andragogical approaches shared in Table 4.1 support the mentee's transition from dependence on the mentor to becoming a self-directed, reflective practitioner capable of navigating the complexities of teaching independently. This is the kind of momentum we seek to build!

Using the lens of Indigenous teachings and the medicine wheel, we all move through four phases of life: beginning as children, then through the struggles of adolescence emerging as adults, and finally seeing the world as elders. This movement is gradual and constant with key people stewarding us through each phase and the associated transitions between them. Just as I (Wayne) needed mentors to help me move through the various stages of my personal life, so did I need significant mentoring through the phases of my educational career. A key part of this was the ability of the mentors to recognize what stage I was at and respond appropriately, matching their approach to my maturity and ability to hear what they were saying.

LAUNCHING INTO MOMENTUM: SURFACE-LEVEL PRACTICES

The Importance of Mentoring Routines

Daily practices are essential for providing ongoing support and fostering the growth of a new teacher. Here are some effective daily practices that mentor teachers can put in place to assist a new teacher. By no means are we suggesting that you attempt every single practice on this list at the same time; rather, we suggest starting with a practice or two that you are already comfortable with and branching out from there. We have included a daily practice tracking tool at the end of the chapter, for you to reflect on the impact of these practices on the momentum of your mentorship.

1. **Morning Touchpoint**
   - **Practice:** Start the day with a brief check-in.
   - **Purpose:** Offer encouragement, address any immediate concerns, and set a positive tone for the day.
   - **Implementation:** Keep it informal and focused on setting goals or addressing specific questions the new teacher might have.
2. **Classroom Walk-Through**
   - **Practice:** Conduct a quick walk-through of the new teacher's classroom during a nondisruptive time.
   - **Purpose:** Provide immediate, in-the-moment feedback and observe how the classroom environment is being managed.
   - **Implementation:** Focus on one or two key areas each day, offering praise and suggestions as needed.
3. **Brief After-Class Reflection**
   - **Practice:** Encourage the new teacher to take 5–10 minutes after each class to reflect on what went well and what could be improved.
   - **Purpose:** Foster a habit of self-reflection and continuous improvement.

- **Implementation:** Provide a simple framework or set of questions for reflection, and discuss these reflections when appropriate.

4. **Daily Planning Support**
   - **Practice:** Spend a few minutes each day reviewing the next day's lesson plans with the new teacher.
   - **Purpose:** Ensure the new teacher feels prepared and confident in their lesson delivery.
   - **Implementation:** Offer suggestions for enhancing the lesson or managing time effectively.
5. **Modeling Classroom Routines**
   - **Practice:** Demonstrate specific classroom routines or management techniques that the new teacher can implement.
   - **Purpose:** Help the new teacher establish consistent classroom procedures.
   - **Implementation:** Show the routine in your classroom or role-play it with the new teacher, then provide support as they implement it.
6. **Quick Debrief at the End of the Day**
   - **Practice:** Have a short debriefing session at the end of each day.
   - **Purpose:** Reflect on the day's events, discuss any challenges, and plan for the next day.
   - **Implementation:** Keep it concise, focusing on one key success and one area for improvement.
7. **Ongoing Resource Provision**
   - **Practice:** Share relevant resources, such as articles, lesson ideas, or classroom materials, that align with the new teacher's needs.
   - **Purpose:** Equip the new teacher with tools that can enhance their teaching.
   - **Implementation:** Tailor the resources to the new teacher's current focus or challenges, and follow up to discuss how they were used.
8. **Daily Encouragement**
   - **Practice:** Offer words of encouragement or positive reinforcement each day.
   - **Purpose:** Boost the new teacher's confidence and morale, especially during challenging times.
   - **Implementation:** Acknowledge small wins, celebrate improvement areas, or simply express appreciation for their hard work.

9. **Focus on One Improvement Area**
    - **Practice:** Identify one specific area for the new teacher to focus on each day (e.g., classroom management, student engagement).
    - **Purpose:** Gradually build the new teacher's skills without overwhelming them.
    - **Implementation:** Provide targeted feedback on this area and offer suggestions for improvement.
10. **Availability for Quick Questions**
    - **Practice:** Make yourself available for quick questions or clarifications throughout the day.
    - **Purpose:** Provide immediate support and reduce the new teacher's stress.
    - **Implementation:** Let the new teacher know when and how they can reach out to you, such as via a quick chat, text, or email.

These daily practices help create a supportive environment where the new teacher feels continuously guided and encouraged. By integrating these routines, mentor teachers can ensure that their mentees develop the skills and confidence needed to thrive in the classroom.

Mentorship Momentum-Building Ideas

Building mentorship momentum is more than simply having the desire to engage in mentorship practices; rather, it is about the deliberate decisions we make as mentors on a daily basis. We must leverage our knowledge of our mentee, as well as maintain a clear understanding of where we are hoping to guide our mentee along. Once we are confident in these, we can then begin to consider more specific mentorship practices intended to help build momentum, progress, and professional growth for our mentees. In conversation with mentors, mentees, and others who are engaged in the mentorship of new and aspiring teachers, we have compiled a short list of practical ideas for you to consider as you continue to build your mentorship momentum:

- Navigating Policies and Procedures
- Long-Term Planning and Goal Setting
- Working With All Professionals in the School

Building mentorship momentum is more than simply having the desire to engage in mentorship practices; rather, it is about the deliberate decisions we make as mentors on a daily basis.

MENTORSHIP MOMENTUM BUILDER #1: NAVIGATING POLICIES AND PROCEDURES

Who wants to learn about policy and procedures? Did you just raise your hand? Great! While this may not sound like as much fun as riding on a roller coaster, helping a new teacher find their way through the various school and district policies and procedures is an important part of immersing them into the profession. From knowing about their teaching contract, to field trip planning, fire drills, lunch supervision, assessment, and calling parents, to learning about the many legal frameworks that underpin education, there are many curves and loop-de-loops to navigate. This can sometimes seem daunting or overwhelming for a new teacher. No one wants to get "in trouble" for not knowing a policy or breaking a rule. Here is where you, as the mentor, can really be of service. Together, let's explore some practical ways to help bring policy and procedures to life and help ease your mentee into what they need to understand, know, and be able to do when it comes to navigating policies and procedures.

Where to Begin

Every new teacher should be familiar with a core set of school policies and procedures to ensure they can effectively manage their classroom, fulfill their professional responsibilities, and contribute to the school community. There are, however, more policies and procedures to consider than can be covered in this section. That said, in Table 4.2 we offer a list of the most common areas that will impact an early career teacher. We recommend using this as a checklist that will help you cover key areas with your mentee.

TABLE 4.2 POLICIES AND PROCEDURES TO EXPLORE WITH YOUR MENTEE

Policies and Procedures to Know	Considerations
1. Classroom Management and Discipline Policies	**Behavior Expectations:** Schoolwide behavior expectations, including the code of conduct for students. **Disciplinary Procedures:** Steps for handling student misbehavior, including referral processes, detention, suspension, and restorative practices. **Positive Behavior Support:** Systems, supports, and routines that promote positive behavior and learner engagement.
2. Grading and Assessment Policies	**Grading and Reporting:** Understanding grading systems, grade weighting, and reporting timelines. **Homework:** Policies on homework expectations, grading late assignments, and providing feedback. **Testing and Assessment:** Guidelines for creating, administering, and grading assessments, including standardized test protocols.
3. Attendance and Tardiness Procedures	**Student Attendance:** Procedures for taking attendance, reporting absences, and dealing with chronic absenteeism. **Teacher Attendance:** Expectations for teacher punctuality, sign-in procedures, and protocols for reporting absences.
4. Safety and Emergency Procedures	**Fire Drills and Lockdowns:** Understanding evacuation routes, lockdown protocols, and emergency response procedures. **Student Safety:** Procedures for handling accidents, injuries, and medical emergencies in the classroom.
5. Communication Protocols	**Parent-Teacher Communication:** Guidelines for communicating with parents, including expectations for responding to emails and conducting conferences. **Internal Communication:** Procedures for communicating with administration, colleagues, and support staff.

(Continued)

(Continued)

Policies and Procedures to Know	Considerations
6. Lesson Planning and Curriculum Requirements	**Lesson Submission:** Procedures for submitting lesson plans for review and adhering to curriculum standards. **Pacing Guides:** Understanding pacing guides, scope and sequence documents, and other planning resources.
7. Technology Use and Policies	**Acceptable Use Policy:** Rules for using school technology, internet access, and digital devices. **Student Privacy Guidelines:** Processes for handling student data and maintaining confidentiality.
8. Special Education and Accommodations	**Individual Education Plans:** Procedures for implementing accommodations and modifications for students with disabilities. **Referral Processes:** Steps for referring students for special education evaluation or additional support services.
9. Professional Conduct and Ethics	**Code of Ethics:** Professional behavior expectations, including dress code, confidentiality, and interactions with students. **Social Media Use:** Guidelines for appropriate use of social media as a teacher.
10. Reporting Procedures	**Child Abuse Reporting:** Mandatory reporting requirements for suspected abuse or neglect. **Bullying and Harassment:** Procedures for reporting bullying incidents and supporting affected students.
11. Substitute Plans and Procedures	**Substitute Folders:** Requirements for providing lesson plans, class rosters, and emergency information for substitute teachers.
12. Field Trip and Extracurricular Activities	**Approval Processes:** Steps to get approval for field trips and necessary paperwork (e.g., permission slips, transportation requests). **Chaperone Expectations:** Guidelines for supervising students during off-campus events.

Policies and Procedures to Know	Considerations
13. Health and Wellness Policies	**Medication Procedures:** How medications are handled at school, including the role of the nurse and teacher responsibilities. **Allergy and Health Concerns:** Awareness of student health plans, such as those for allergies, asthma, or other chronic conditions.
14. State and Other Government Policies	**Professional Practice Standards:** These provide the competencies and skills expected of teachers. **Other:** Antidiscrimination laws, occupational health and safety, certification and licensing requirements, and other policies pertinent to your context.

Again, we offer this table as a starting point. There will be other important policies, procedures, and state legislation to consider. Consulting with your school leadership team is a great way to coordinate your efforts to ensure that key school policies are covered. So, now that we have thought about what to cover, let's next explore how you explore policies and procedures with your mentee.

How to Engage With Your Mentee

One of the great aspects of independent approaches to mentoring is that you as the mentor get to learn as well. By unpacking policies and procedures with your mentee, you get the value-added bonus of refreshing and even deepening your praxis with policy. The issue is how to effectively cover all of the required matter.

A suggestion, based on Indigenous practices, is to embed multiple ideas in what is being discussed—the theoretical and the practical. This will make the time spent both relevant and useful to the "future" teacher you are mentoring. When young people are taught to hunt, many ideas such as stewardship of the land and animals are discussed alongside the practicalities of tracking, harvesting, and preparing the animals. When the mentee is finally successful in their efforts, the teachings that have been embedded are instantly applicable and do not need to be taught separately. In other words, the "why" has been embedded in the process.

With so much to consider and unpack, we recommend that you go slowly. Select only one or two policies at a time to discuss. Think of it like eating a fruitcake. Pick a little piece, nibble, savor, and then come back for another piece. In time, you will cover the key areas and have had time to digest the relevant knowledge and teacher responsibilities pertinent to each policy. Here are eight approaches that we invite you to try with your mentee in nibbling away at policies and procedures.

1. **Personalized Guidance and Conversations**
   - **One-to-One Meetings:** Schedule regular meetings to discuss school policies, share personal experiences, and answer questions.
   - **Focused Discussions:** Break down policies into manageable topics (e.g., grading, discipline, communication with parents) and discuss each in depth.
2. **Modeling and Demonstration**
   - **Modeling Best Practices:** Demonstrate how policies are implemented in real classroom situations, such as how to conduct parent–teacher conferences or manage classroom behavior.
   - **Shadowing Opportunities:** Allow the new teacher to shadow you (the mentor) in various school settings (staff meetings, student interactions) to see policies in action.
3. **Providing Resources**
   - **Create a Resource Binder:** Compile a binder or digital folder with essential documents like the staff handbook, discipline guidelines, and lesson planning templates.
   - **Scenario-Based Guides:** Provide practical examples and scenarios that illustrate how to handle specific situations according to school policies.
4. **Role-Playing and Simulations**
   - **Simulated Scenarios:** Use role-playing to practice responding to real-life situations, such as handling a disruptive student or dealing with an upset parent, while adhering to school policies.
   - **Feedback Sessions:** After simulations, provide constructive feedback to help the new teacher refine their approach.

5. **Ongoing Support and Check-Ins**
   - **Regular Check-Ins:** Schedule check-ins to review how the new teacher is applying policies in the classroom and to address any challenges they may be facing.
   - **Reflection Opportunities:** Encourage the new teacher to reflect on their experiences and share insights or questions about policies they find challenging.
6. **Access to School Culture and Networks**
   - **Introduce Key Staff Members:** Connect the new teacher with other staff members who can provide insights into specific policies (e.g., guidance counselors, administrators).
   - **Encourage Participation in School Committees:** Get the new teacher involved in committees or teams where they can see policy discussions and decisions in action.
7. **Visual Aids and Cheat Sheets**
   - **Quick Reference Guides:** Create cheat sheets with key points of important procedures, like emergency protocols, attendance policies, or reporting requirements.
   - **Visual Flowcharts:** Use flowcharts to outline processes, making them easier to understand and follow.
8. **Mentorship Journal or Log**
   - **Document Learning:** Encourage the new teacher to keep a journal or log of their learning about policies and procedures, noting any questions or reflections.
   - **Action Plans:** Work together to develop action plans for how the new teacher will implement what they've learned.

These approaches help your mentee understand not only the "what" and "how" of school policies but also the "why," making the learning process more engaging and applicable. Again, while this might not necessarily feel like fast-paced momentum-building work, you are truly pouring the foundation of the rules, regulations, statutes, and legal frameworks that the profession is built upon. Ensuring your mentee understands what is expected of them in policy and procedure is helpful for their success and in helping to retain them in the profession. To gain a greater sense of the impact you are having with these approaches, be sure to check in with your mentee for their feedback. Confirmation questions are helpful to gauge their understanding.

QUESTIONS TO ASK YOUR MENTEE

Here is a bank of sample questions that you could use to precipitate conversations on a variety of policies:

1. Describe the key steps you will follow when a student repeatedly disrupts the class.
2. Can you describe the protocol for requesting time off or handling sick days?
3. How do you ensure compliance with policies regarding student accommodations?
4. What are the school's guidelines for professional conduct and interactions with students, parents, and colleagues?
5. Explain the steps you will take if a student shares something with you that raises a concern for their safety.
6. What are the school's expectations for lesson planning, submission deadlines, and classroom observations?
7. What procedures should you follow when planning a parent–teacher conference, and how do you document these interactions?

Remember, given that many new teachers come with experience from other fields (i.e., teaching is their second or third career), it is important to ask what they already know and understand about the policies and procedures. Having them explain what they know can more readily help you press into the areas where they need to go and grow in their knowledge and understanding.

MENTORSHIP MOMENTUM BUILDER #2: LONG-TERM PLANNING AND GOAL SETTING

Long-term planning and goal setting are often aspects of the mentor–mentee relationship that can be overlooked, especially when we consider the intentional purpose behind long-term planning. In general, we recommend that mentors engage in a conversation with mentees regarding the purpose of these types of plans, and clarify specifically what the plans are intended for versus how the mentee is meant to understand their purpose. Many new teachers do not receive adequate training in the difference between lesson planning, unit planning, and long-term planning.

We propose that a necessary clarification of the importance of long-term plans will build momentum for your mentee. Remember that impactful long-term planning is less about specific details and more about understanding the timeline and the ebb and flow of a school year. As someone who has spent time in the classroom, we rarely even consider the fact that a school year has an ebb and flow; rather, it is just a natural part of our experience. Thus, the first step in assisting our mentee with long-term plans is to communicate the general flow of the school year and how it impacts teaching.

Communicating high-priority instructional events. It is imperative we talk to our mentees about events like end-of-semester reporting cutoffs, parent–teacher conferences, gradebook deadlines, state or provincial assessment dates, and so on. Having these events scheduled in the calendar will hide any surprises for our mentees, and will allow them to coordinate their instructional and assessment calendars accordingly. There is nothing worse for a mentee than the realization that an end-of-semester gradebook cutoff is only a few days away when there is still a pile of assignments to be graded.

Communicating immovable calendar events. Ensure you discuss and include holidays, professional learning days, noninstructional meeting days, staff meeting days, and so on. Being a new teacher is already difficult enough, so by reminding your mentee to include these events in their long-term planning, you will hopefully mitigate some panicked late arrivals to staff meetings or school gatherings!

Balancing Different Approaches to Long-Term Planning

An important aspect to remember as we guide our mentees through the planning process is that no two teachers plan the same. What is prioritized in the planning process, the methods and ideologies considered in the process, and the tools used to help the process are often attributed to what each individual person values. Thus, keeping an open mind about these things will allow for a smoother planning conversation as the goal for all of us (regardless of the process we use) is to be as prepared as possible for instruction. As such, we wanted to establish some norms and realities that must be considered by all who engage in long-term planning. Our role as mentors, then, is to ensure our mentees are aware of the following critical messages.

We should be fluent in understanding the delicate balance between standards (outcomes) and curriculum. What we mean by this is ensuring that we always use our standards or outcomes as the compass that should guide our planning. These are the non-negotiables that can be easily overlooked in the planning process. Curriculum is important but should always be measured against our standards and outcomes to ensure we are addressing all that we are required to address. It is very tempting and easy for new teachers to want to simply follow a book page by page, yet we must communicate to our mentees that not all standards and outcomes are created equally and thus long-term planning is less about the order of delivery and more about understanding when we should go deeper in the instruction of certain standards and outcomes.

We should be deliberate in communicating the importance of mastery of student learning. A critical aspect of long-term planning is ensuring our mentee understands the importance of scaffolding their instruction and assessment to ensure a progression toward mastery. Long-term planning will be more impactful if our mentees can envision a road map to mastery for their students. This road map to mastery should include an understanding of how we will formatively assess students' progress and adjust instruction as necessary. It should also include how students will show mastery through summative assessment practices. As the more experienced colleague, it will be our role to ensure clarity of understanding and guidance for our mentee as they consider instruction and assessment practices to promote mastery across a school year.

We should maintain a critical lens when sharing and using resources. Teachers newer to the profession tend to assume that all resources are of high value, when the reality is most often the opposite. Not all resources are created equally, and just because there might be a price tag attached to the resource does not make it more valuable than others. As mentors, we need to be able to help our mentees develop a critical eye to determine what is a valuable resource, and what might be a resource that looks good but does not really have much substance. Similarly, it does not do much benefit for us to simply turn over every single resource and document we use all at once. I (Vince) remember receiving unlimited access to a colleague's drive, and it took me longer to sift through and find something I would use than to build something of my own. We aren't saying we should not share resources, but we must be cautious to not overshare and overwhelm our mentees with our generosity. After all, we will have a greater impact if we can share our strategies for determining what makes a great resource.

Using Long-Term Plans to Collaboratively Set Goals

As we engage with our mentees in the long-term planning process, this is also a great time to collaboratively set goals for the school year. Having a few yearlong goals for our mentees to strive toward will be beneficial in framing our future conversations and observations. We have included a template in Figure 4.1 that can be used as you engage in goal setting with your mentee.

Figure 4.1 • Yearlong Goal-Setting Template

<table>
<tr><td colspan="2">Yearlong Goal:</td></tr>
<tr><td>Checkpoints to Success
•
•
•
•</td><td>How will I know when I have met the goal?</td></tr>
<tr><td colspan="2">What are my next steps?</td></tr>
</table>

The purpose of this template is to establish a consistent approach to assist us in the cocreation of a tangible goal. You will notice the Checkpoints to Success section. In this section it is our hope that you and your mentee will establish midpoint markers for growth and progress as your mentee trends toward meeting their goal. The purpose of the two reflection questions is to encourage metacognition for our mentees to reflect upon what success will look like, and then subsequently determine their next steps. It is our hope that this template will be used to frame formal and informal observations, as well as mentor and mentee meetings.

While there is no set number to be created, we recommend establishing two or three goals per year. Each goal is intended to reflect a different area of mastery (instructional, assessment practices, classroom environment, etc.). Ultimately, this yields its greatest impact when both mentor and mentee are able to reflect on the journey of the mentee using this document as a common conversation piece. The value is in the mentor being able to use their expertise to help the mentee navigate to success. We unpack this idea further in the next chapter when we discuss leveling up and letting go.

QUESTIONS TO ASK YOUR MENTEE

1. How are you currently prioritizing and organizing your long-term plans?
2. Where are you currently accessing your resources to support your teaching? How do you ensure that these resources are of the highest quality?
3. To what extent are you familiar with your standards and curriculum? How might you organize these to ensure the most important ones are addressed?

MENTORSHIP MOMENTUM BUILDER #3: WORKING WITH ALL PROFESSIONALS IN THE SCHOOL

The environment in which we work directly impacts how we work. A positive school culture with belonging as a central tenet of our day-to-day actions is vital for engaging and retaining not only students but staff as well. Very few people want to work in a building that is devoid of relationships. Positive school environments enhance student engagement by fostering a positive atmosphere where students feel safe, valued, and motivated. The same holds true for staff. As a teacher, we must remember that all of our coworkers deserve to feel part of the team.

When belonging and respect is a cornerstone of school culture, everyone is more likely to engage actively, collaborate effectively, and take risks in their learning. Such environments promote emotional well-being, reduce behavioral issues, and create a supportive space where we can all thrive academically and personally. Respect among teachers, staff, and students builds strong relationships, which are essential for effective teaching and learning. Overall, a respectful school environment lays the foundation for academic success and personal growth.

Building effective working relationships with nonteaching staff is crucial for creating a harmonious and productive school environment. Here are five pieces of advice to help a new teacher connect with educational assistants, custodial staff, and secretarial staff:

1. **Show Respect and Appreciation:** Always acknowledge the important roles nonteaching staff play. A simple "thank you" or a note of appreciation for their hard work can go a long way. Recognizing their efforts in meetings as well as informally is important. Always remember that all of these people have expertise and a desire to do a good job.
2. **Communicate Clearly and Regularly:** Open and honest communication is essential. Share your classroom plans and needs with educational assistants and custodial staff to ensure they understand how they can support the students and the activities in the classroom. Help build a team in your classroom of caring and committed adults.
3. **Set Clear Expectations:** Be clear in outlining what you need from nonteaching staff. Being clear about your expectations helps avoid misunderstandings and fosters a more efficient working relationship.
4. **Listen Actively:** Value everyone's input and feedback. Nonteaching staff will have valuable insights into student needs, school history, and activities. Listening to their

perspectives not only improves your working relationship but also enhances your effectiveness as a teacher.

5. **Be Flexible and Understanding:** Nonteaching staff have their own responsibilities and constraints to contend with. Being adaptable and understanding of their schedules and workloads will help in building mutual respect and cooperation.

A Few More Thoughts

Spending time teaching your mentee how to work with and embrace their colleagues and coworkers as valuable sources of strength and inspiration is crucial for building their own ability to be a resilient, participating member of the staff. Recognizing colleagues as individuals who contribute positively to mental wellness can significantly enhance a mentee's professional experience and personal well-being.

Working over the year to encourage your mentee to view their colleagues not just as coworkers but as people with diverse experiences, skills, and perspectives is vitally important to them being viewed as the same. Emphasize that everyone in the school community brings strengths and insight that can be helpful in navigating the challenges of teaching. For instance, learning how a colleague's coping strategies, their problem-solving skills, or even their approaches to work–life balance work for them can offer valuable lessons and practical advice for your mentee.

Promoting a balanced dialogue about mental wellness with your mentee can help them understand where they are in relation to their colleagues and encourage a global view of the staff they work with. When colleagues share their own experiences and coping mechanisms, it normalizes the conversation around mental health and reduces stigma. Encourage your mentee to engage in these conversations, seek advice, and offer support in return. This mutual exchange of ideas and encouragement creates a culture of empathy and collective resilience.

By guiding your mentee to build meaningful relationships and value their colleagues as sources of strength and inspiration, you help them develop a strong support network that enhances their resilience and helps them contribute and benefit from a strong resilient school community.

Rounding the Bases of Mentorship Momentum

Earlier in this chapter we invited you to press play on your favorite "walk-up" song and step up to the plate for some mentorship momentum–building ideas. What is your song? Is it a fast-paced rocker like "Kickstart My Heart" (Mötley Crüe, 1989) or perhaps a melodic motivator like "Take on Me" (A-ha, 1985)? Maybe you selected something a little more chill like "Three Little Birds" (Marley, 1977). In any case, the tempo, the feel, and the beat are all part of the big push of this chapter, which is how to build momentum with your mentee. Building mentorship momentum is about creating a sustainable and evolving relationship that benefits the mentee, the mentor, and, ultimately, the students. To maintain this momentum, mentors must remain responsive, proactive, and open to new ideas. Through the lens of andragogy, a mentor needs to encourage mentees to take ownership of their development while providing a supportive space for exploration, experimentation, and even failure—because every experience is an opportunity to grow.

As a mentor, your role is not to provide all the answers, but to help your mentee find their own solutions. Through reflective practices, shared experiences, and honest dialogue, you empower them to develop their teaching philosophy and approach. You are there to guide them in navigating challenges and to celebrate their successes. Remember that with the T.I.M.E. approaches we shared in Chapter 2, there are many ways to engage with your mentee. You need to find the ones that give you that momentum moving forward.

True mentorship is about recognizing that growth is a continuous process. Even as the formal mentoring relationship comes to a close, the seeds you've planted continue to grow, impacting the mentee's future as a teacher. It's not the end of the journey but the beginning of their independence and confidence as educators.

As discussed previously, in Indigenous culture people move through phases of life, gaining and gathering skills along the way, eventually becoming elders. Mentors and mentees will do that too—each moving toward becoming the master teacher they desire to be. It is important to note that even master teachers need others to talk to and seek guidance from when encountering challenges. Having a mentee eventually be there for the mentor is not an oddity; it in fact is a desired thing—as it means the mentoring has worked!

As you move forward, remember that the most successful mentoring relationships are those that encourage risk-taking, resilience, and innovation. Continue to check in with your mentee, foster an open line of communication, and stay curious about their progress. Let this relationship evolve beyond the formal structure into a professional network of support and encouragement.

Ultimately, your mentorship has the power to create a ripple effect—not only in your mentee's career but in the lives of the students they will impact. When you help a mentee grow into a more effective and reflective teacher, you contribute to a stronger, more vibrant educational community. Keep pushing forward, and know that your efforts will continue to shape the future of teaching and learning. Like the roller coaster we referenced at the outset of this chapter, enjoy the ups and downs, the twists and turns, and, most of all, the relationships you build with our next generation of teachers.

Like all exciting rides, we need to stop now and again to ensure all the parts are working, and that the structures are intact. In the next chapter, we will share ideas on how to maintain your work as a mentor and know when to make those necessary adjustments to keep momentum going.

UNPACKING OUR ABCDs OF MENTORSHIP MOMENTUM

In Chapter 1, we spent some time addressing the importance of unpacking our *attitudes, biases, conceptual understanding,* and *dispositions* (ABCDs) toward mentorship. We offer two provocations for your reflection and consideration:

1. Having read this chapter on mentorship momentum, what are your ABCDs toward the ideas we have shared? Use the space provided to jot down three ideas that have resonated most with you.

Idea 1.
Idea 2.
Idea 3.

2. With a colleague, share a momentum-building idea from this chapter that you will commit to trying with your mentee.

DAILY PRACTICE TRACKING TOOL

Earlier in the chapter we presented you with 10 daily practices you can try to build your mentorship momentum. Choose two practices and use the space provided to reflect upon the purpose and implementation of each.

Daily Practice #1:	
Reflection on Purpose:	Reflection on Implementation:
Daily Practice #2:	
Reflection on Purpose:	Reflection on Implementation:

CHAPTER FIVE

Maintaining Mentorship

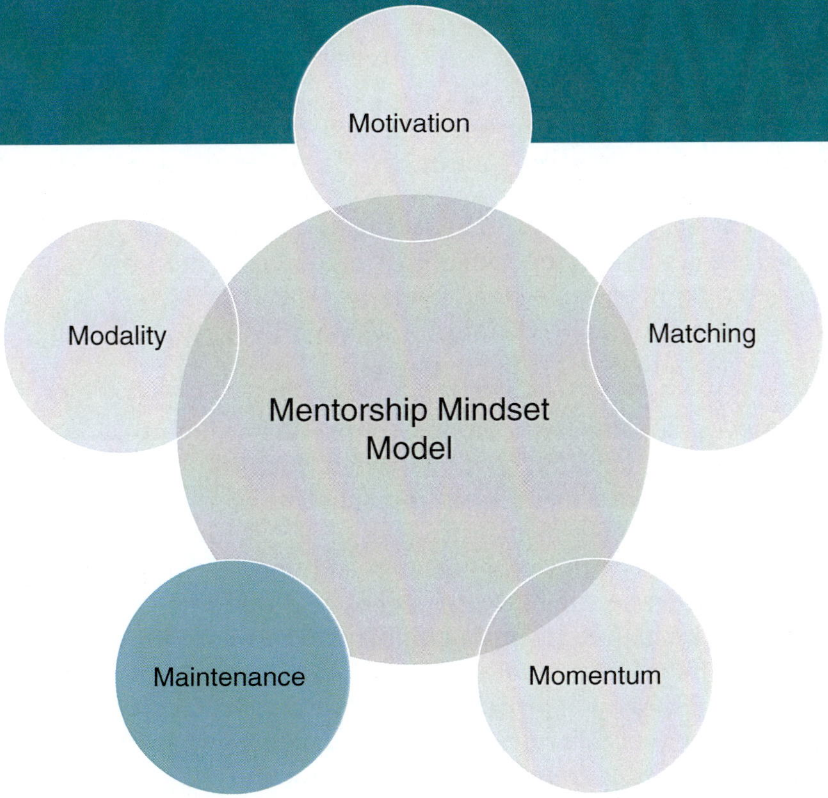

Motivation

Modality

Matching

Mentorship Mindset Model

Maintenance

Momentum

The place to improve the world is first in one's own heart and head, and hands, and then work outward from there.

— Robert M. Pirsig (1975, p. 305)

In Chapter 4, we explored how to convert our mentorship potential into kinetic actions that build momentum between mentor and mentee. Like a motorcycle rolling swiftly along an open roadway, we balance where we are with where we started and where we wish to be. To this point, we like to think that the motorcycle has a sidecar. You, as the mentor, have been sitting in the sidecar, offering sage advice and guidance, while your mentee has been learning to drive and effectively operate the vehicle. Like all good things, there comes a time when the mentor must step back a bit and let the mentee assume more responsibility. Maintaining the dynamic between mentor and mentee is what this chapter will explore. What comes to mind when you see the word *maintenance*?

Words are amazing things. From their dictionary meaning (denotation) to their emotive capability to affect our feelings (connotation), we know that it is the power of language (spoken and written) that propels our relationships and learning forward. If we look up the word *maintenance* in a dictionary (Oxford University Press, 2025), we observe that it is a noun that has several meanings:

- The act of making a state or situation continue
- The act of keeping something in good condition by checking or repairing it regularly
- The resources needed for somebody's living expenses; the act of providing these resources

Maintenance also has a French connection to the word *maintenant*, which means "now." So, when we think about the need to maintain our mentorship momentum, we must also think about the long-term maintenance of the mentoring relationship we have with our mentee. In addition, we must consider the resources of time, effort, energy, and care that go into the pairing as an investment in our mentee. Furthermore, when we recall the *traditional*, *interdependent*, *metacognitive*, and *environmental* (T.I.M.E.) approaches to mentoring (see Chapter 2), we seek a reciprocal investment from our mentee whereby we can grow and learn from them. So we now find ourselves at the point in the book where we are going to explore the art of mentorship maintenance (and, hopefully, a little Zen).

In this chapter, we will examine approaches and techniques that will help both you and your mentee to move forward. This includes how to gradually ease back and let your mentee assume more responsibility as well as techniques to keep the relationship moving with opportunities for check-ins to address items needing repair and to celebrate milestones and successes.

MENTORSHIP MAINTENANCE IDEAS

Mentorship maintenance is about providing an appropriate amount of space to allow your mentee the opportunity to make mistakes, learn, and develop their own capacities in the classroom. The following section is intended to provide you with a few ideas to consider that will help you maintain the mentorship balance that exists, and even restore a sense of efficacy in your mentee:

- Realities of Mentorship
- Creating Opportunities for Additional Support
- Leveling Up and Letting Go
- Feedback and Expert Noticing to Promote Mastery

Mentorship Maintenance Idea #1: Realities of Mentorship

Your role as a mentor is naturally ever changing, and as such there will be cases where you will have to go with the flow, so to speak. This can be true in the case of a mentee. What we mean by this is that there may be a time or two where your personality and the personality of your mentee do not jibe as naturally as others. This is a reality of working in a career with lots of different people from different backgrounds and experiences, with their own unique personality types. Whereas in Chapter 3 we focused on mentorship matching and the importance of fit, we know that you may experience a different type of mentoring relationship that, ultimately, you will be required (or tasked) to maintain. So, let's explore some ideas that will help keep you attuned to your mentorship reality.

FORMAL VS. INFORMAL MENTORSHIP

An aspect of mentorship that we must navigate is the idea of formal and informal mentoring relationships, and how we may or may not factor into both relationships with our mentee.

Formal mentoring relationships are established when the mentor and mentee are placed together by an organization or organizational leader. In these cases, the mentee does not choose the person who will be their mentor. On the other hand, informal mentoring relationships are established in a manner where the mentee has more autonomy over who they solicit advice from. As follows you will find a list of formal and informal relationships; as you read through the list, take time to reflect upon your current mentee(s) and the relationship you have with them.

FORMAL MENTORING RELATIONSHIPS

- **Assigned Mentor Programs:** Schools often assign an experienced teacher to mentor new hires. These mentors provide structured guidance on curriculum planning, classroom management, and professional development.
- **Peer Observation Programs:** Some schools have formal peer observation initiatives, where new teachers observe veteran teachers in action and then meet to discuss teaching strategies and classroom techniques.
- **District-Sponsored Induction Programs**: Many districts offer formal induction programs for new teachers. These programs often include workshops, regular check-ins with a mentor, and assessments to ensure new teachers are adjusting well to their roles.
- **Professional Learning Communities (PLCs)**: These are formal groups of educators who meet regularly to collaborate on teaching practices and student learning. New teachers benefit from the support and shared experiences within these structured communities.

INFORMAL MENTORING RELATIONSHIPS

- **Coffee or Lunch Chats With Veteran Teachers:** Informal conversations over lunch or coffee with experienced teachers can offer new teachers a chance to ask questions, share experiences, and receive advice on various teaching challenges in a relaxed setting.
- **Grade-Level or Subject Teams:** In many schools, teachers of the same grade or subject naturally develop a support system where they share resources, lesson plans, and teaching strategies without the structure of formal mentorship.

- **Social Media Teacher Communities:** Many new teachers find mentorship through social media groups or forums where they can ask questions, share ideas, and receive encouragement from more experienced teachers globally.
- **Spontaneous Classroom Visits:** A more informal approach could involve new teachers dropping by experienced colleagues' classrooms for advice or help with a specific challenge they're facing. These ad hoc visits foster a less structured, more organic form of mentorship.

Mentorship maintenance is about understanding the role you play and the dynamic of your relationship with your mentee. In many cases, informal mentoring relationships exist between peers, which in some cases may not include you directly. It is important for us to not force this dynamic and rather understand our role and purpose in supporting our mentees. Allowing our mentees to explore other informal mentorship opportunities will promote their ability to seek out support from others once the formal mentorship time ends. Informal mentorship offers a safe space for mentees to build their efficacy and the collective efficacy of their peers as they engage in problem solving, resource sharing, and conversation in a more horizontal manner. In certain cases, informal opportunities can arise from simple life experiences that align individuals who hold common interests and passions.

Wayne reminds us that Indigenous ways of knowing yield organic opportunities for informal mentorship experiences. He shares the following: Many years ago, when I (Wayne) lived in a northwestern Canada community, I watched a master Tsimshian carver take a large cedar log and slowly turn it into a totem pole. During that time, a number of high school–aged students came down to the carving shed to watch. As the students looked on, the carver kept working, carving away at his cedar log. As he noticed certain students showing interest, he would invite them to try and use the tools. Many students only came once, a few came back more often, and eventually some of them became his apprentice carvers, becoming mentees to the master carver.

VERTICAL AND HORIZONTAL MENTORSHIP

It is clear in the literature that vertical mentorship, or what many would recognize as the traditional notion of a more experienced mentor leading the less experienced mentee, is best augmented by horizontal mentoring, or mentees working together to "figure it out" themselves. This hybrid can best be illustrated in this scenario:

MENTORSHIP MOMENT

Ms. Nguyen, a seasoned teacher and mentor, sat down in the staff room with her two mentees, Alex and Jordan. She noticed the determined looks on their faces and sensed they had something important to share.

"Ah," Alex began, "we've been struggling with classroom management, especially during group activities. But instead of coming straight to you for answers, Jordan and I decided to brainstorm together."

Jordan nodded. "We realized we could support each other by sharing what works and doesn't work in our classrooms. We started by watching each other's classes and taking notes on student behavior and engagement. Then each night after school we met up to discuss what we saw."

Ms. Nguyen smiled, encouraging them to continue.

"We found that the students were more engaged when we set clear expectations and consistently followed through with consequences," Alex explained. "Jordan suggested we create a set of classroom norms together with the students, so they have a sense of ownership."

"Yeah, and we remembered what you said about engaging parents and caregivers," Jordan added. "We've been making calls to tell them all the good things that are going on and how their child is growing. We've concentrated on keeping it positive, and it's been working well so far, and the students are really responding positively."

Ms. Nguyen nodded approvingly. "It sounds like you two have developed a solid plan by collaborating and reflecting on your experiences. How has it felt working together as peers?"

"It's been empowering," Jordan said. "We've learned a lot from each other, and it feels good to know we're not alone in this."

"Absolutely," Alex agreed. "We've both grown as teachers by tackling these challenges together."

Ms. Nguyen beamed with pride. "I'm so impressed with your initiative and teamwork. By supporting each other, you're not just finding solutions—you're building a strong foundation for your teaching careers. I'm happy to hear you were able to incorporate my suggestion. Keep up the great work, and remember, I'm always here if you need guidance."

Both horizontal and vertical mentorship can be powerful tools for growth. Whichever model or hybrid of the two is deemed to be the chosen strategy, it is important that community is developed between all involved to provide the emotional capital that will be needed during the moments of trial and tribulation.

RELATIONSHIP BUILDING IS THE KEY TO FORMAL AND INFORMAL MENTORSHIP

Building strong relationships between mentors and mentees is essential for the success of any mentoring program. Effective relationship building fosters trust, open communication, and mutual respect, which are crucial for the mentee's professional and personal development. Here are some activities that mentors can engage in to strengthen their relationship-building skills with their mentees.

REGULAR CHECK-IN MEETINGS

It's hard to establish a relationship with someone you do not see or just wave to as you pass in a crowded hallway on the way to the photocopier. Therefore, it is important to schedule regular one-to-one meetings with your mentee, such as weekly or biweekly check-ins, to provide a regular, structured opportunity to discuss progress, challenges, and goals. These meetings help mentors and mentees to establish a routine and create a safe space for open and honest communication.

Hold the meetings in a neutral space where you are both comfortable and encourage your mentee to bring their questions and items to celebrate. While there may not always be a great deal to talk about, it will give you an opportunity to continue to build your relationship.

COLLABORATIVE GOAL SETTING

During your meetings, build in time to work together to set and maintain short-term and long-term goals for the mentee. This collaborative goal setting involves the mentee in their development plan, ensuring that the goals are aligned with their aspirations and interests, and keeps it from just being a prescriptive activity where the mentor informs the mentee on their next steps. This activity promotes a sense of ownership and motivation. The goals should be clear but written in pencil rather than ink as they will evolve and change over time. Supporting the goals with ways to capture data for measurement so that the mentee has a sense of their growth and if they are moving toward (or away from) the goal is important.

SOCIAL AND INFORMAL ACTIVITIES

One of the best leaders I (Wayne) have worked under was fond of saying "it's the mortar, not the bricks," that's important in keeping a team together, functioning at a high level. The moments in the staff room or going out for some wings after a particularly hard week help build the mortar, the human connections that allow us to get through the hard times together. Becoming best friends is not the goal, but knowing when someone's birthday is, or that they have kids and a partner (or not) to get home to, is important. Many mentees want to know they are cared about beyond just as a colleague. Time spent getting to know each other is never wasted time!

The most challenging aspect of navigating the dynamics of your relationship will be knowing when to provide support and when to provide space for your mentee to discover things on their own. We recommend keeping an open conversation and prompting more discovery opportunities using some of the following questions.

QUESTIONS TO ASK YOUR MENTEE

1. Have you considered joining an online or in-person community of your peers who are also in their first year of teaching? What lessons have you taken from your peers that have impacted your practice this year?
2. What can I do better to ensure you are getting the most value out of our mentor-mentee relationship?
3. Do you have questions about district services or support that I can possibly answer for you?

Mentorship Maintenance Idea #2: Creating Opportunities for Additional Support

Nothing in schools is as constant as change! Due to teacher shortages, we are seeing more and more teachers moving from school to school—serving wherever they are needed in their district. Thus, a mentor's role extends beyond providing immediate guidance and support; it also involves helping a mentee build a strong network of colleagues in and outside of their current school community. It is also important to remind mentors that many of you took on this work in an effort to "future proof" your school and profession by helping strengthen teachers with less experience to become strong, resilient teachers capable of moving forward. This strategic approach is crucial for the mentee's professional growth and long-term career development, as it reduces their reliance on the mentor and prepares them to navigate their future as it unfolds.

1. **Expanding Professional Horizons:** By assisting the mentee to grow their network with colleagues in and outside the school, a mentor helps them gain perspectives and new ways of looking at challenges. Interacting with other teachers from different backgrounds, specialties, and schools can expose the mentee to new ideas, teaching methods, and practices. This broader perspective grows their skill set and makes them more able to meet new challenges that arise.
2. **Building Support Systems:** A well-rounded network provides a safety net of support and resources. Colleagues

within the school can offer immediate assistance and insights related to the specific context of their institution, while connections outside the school can provide broader industry knowledge, innovative practices, and potential collaboration opportunities. This network ensures that the mentee has access to a wide array of support, reducing their dependency on the mentor alone.

3. **Enhancing Problem-Solving Abilities:** Having connections with a range of educators beyond their mentor provides the mentee with multiple approaches to solving challenges. Learning to seek advice from various sources, as well as growing their critical thinking and problem-solving skills, is important to long-term success.
4. **Creating Opportunities for Professional Growth:** A variety of professional opportunities, including workshops, conferences, and collaborative projects, exist if mentees are able to move beyond their areas of comfort. A good mentor helps mentees realize this and make moves to support this growth.
5. **Building Independence and Confidence:** As the mentee grows their network, they become less dependent on their mentor for support and guidance. This independence fosters confidence in their abilities to navigate their career and solve challenges on their own. They learn to leverage their network for advice and support, thereby developing a sense of autonomy and self-reliance, growing from mentee–mentor to a more mutual relationship.

Helping a mentee grow their professional network during their first year of teaching is crucial for their development and success. Here's a focused idea to consider:

Introduce: Begin by taking time to intentionally introduce your mentee to colleagues within the school. Facilitate initial meetings with experienced teachers, department heads, and other staff members and look for opportunities to create groups of mentees who can grow together. Make sure to highlight each contact's areas of expertise and suggest specific topics for discussion. This personal introduction can make networking less intimidating and more productive.

Encourage: Help your mentee find opportunities to engage in school events, committees, and professional development workshops. Active participation in a variety of school activities provides opportunities to meet and connect with a broad network of educators and professionals.

Promote: Take some time to assist your mentee in joining local or national teaching organizations related to their subject area or interests. These organizations often offer networking events, online forums, and conferences that can expand their professional connections and provide additional resources and support. They can be the same as or different from the ones you are part of.

Leverage: Guide your mentee to create and maintain an appropriate professional presence on educational social media and career platforms. Encourage them to follow educational leaders, join relevant groups, and participate respectfully in online discussions. Social media is a powerful tool for connecting with other educators and staying updated on industry trends.

Goal Setting: Work with your mentee to set specific goals, such as attending a certain number of events or reaching out to specific individuals. Revisit these goals regularly and adjust them to keep the mentee motivated and focused on expanding their network.

GONE FISHING

Imagine a fishing guide helping a novice fisherman discover a few productive fishing spots. The guide knows the best locations, understands the patterns of the fish, and provides valuable tips for a successful catch. Similarly, a mentor assists a mentee in finding a network of like-minded educators by leveraging their own experience and connections.

Just as the guide takes the fisherman to prime spots where fish are likely to bite, the mentor introduces the mentee to key educational communities and professionals who align with their interests and goals. They might point the mentee toward relevant professional organizations, conferences, or online forums where they can connect with educators who share similar passions and challenges.

The mentor also offers insights into navigating these networks, much like the guide shares techniques for casting and reeling. They advise on how to approach conversations, seek out collaborative opportunities, and build meaningful relationships. By guiding their mentee through these steps, the mentor ensures that the mentee can find their own productive "fishing spots" within the educational community, establishing connections that will support their growth and success. This strategic guidance helps the mentee cast their net wide and effectively, leading to a richer, more rewarding professional experience.

Mentorship Maintenance Idea #3: Leveling Up and Letting Go

As with anything we learn in life such as riding a bike, driving a car, or scuba diving, we may have learned vicariously through watching others, but we most likely had someone help us to learn the various components (subskills) needed to master the competencies inherent to each skill. This more experienced other was probably highly involved (hands-on) at the outset but, as we demonstrated growing efficacy with the task, gradually stepped back, allowing us to assert our newly honed skills.

Moving from a novice level of understanding and performance to a level of mastery, especially as a teacher, takes time. From completing a university education program to entering a school system as a new teacher, we know it takes several years for a person to truly flourish in the art, craft, and science of great teaching and learning. Beyond onboarding and induction, we need minimally three and preferably five years to really help the new teacher to grow into the profession. As we articulated early in the book, we are not retaining new teachers long enough in many instances to help them reach a professional functioning point that allows them to not merely survive but also thrive and hopefully flourish. As a mentor, you are truly helping to create the conditions to help retain the teachers we need. So now, we will share a model that will help you move your mentee along the track toward mastery.

In Tim and Vince's book *Leader Ready: Four Pathways to Prepare Aspiring School Leaders* (Cusack & Bustamante, 2023), we shared a skill development model that is predicated on a gradual release of responsibility. Stemming from inspiration that Tim had while learning to scuba dive a few years ago, we devised a leveled model that moves the learner from a surface level of understanding to a deeper level of learning and growth toward mastery. We share a mentorship version of the model with you here (see Figure 5.1, page 125) as it is very helpful in equipping

Figure 5.1 ◆ Levels of Experience Model

Mentor Guidance
Level 3
Level 2
Level 1
Student–Parent–Teacher Conferences
Release of Responsibility

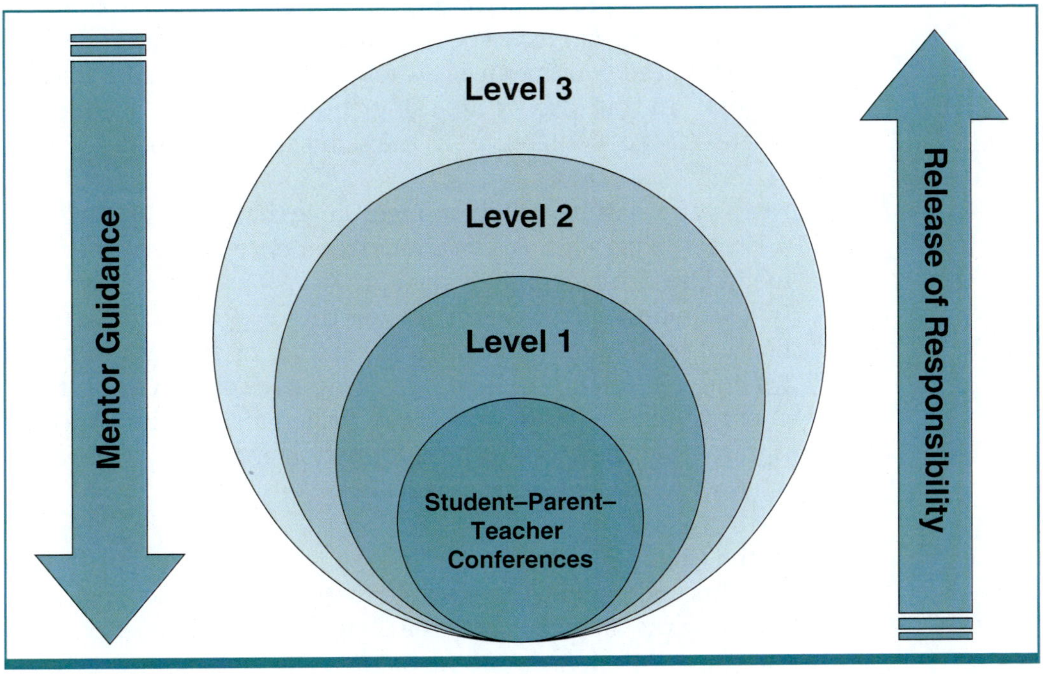

you to realize greater capacity for skill attainment in your mentee. This model helps you to understand where and when more hands-on support is needed and when to ease back and let the mentee fully take the wheel.

LEVELS OF EXPERIENCE MODEL

Imagine learning to scuba dive—going from never having been more than a few feet underwater when swimming or snorkeling to being 100 feet below the surface. Sound scary? Perhaps exciting? It is both. This is how our mentees can feel when learning a new task or skills required of them. Thus, we don't want to put them in over their head to start. Rather, we want to dip our toes in the shallow end first and then dive deeper. Through the trust, respect, and clear guidance you offer your mentee, our model will help you to better help your mentee to move from novice level to proficiency and ultimately, in time, mastery. Let's dive right in, shall we?

Take a look at Figure 5.1. What you observe is four circles overlaying each other. The smallest circle is the skill or concept you want your mentee to learn. It might be a policy, a procedure, a pedagogical approach, a way of taking attendance, a questioning technique, or what have you. Essentially, it is the concept or skill that you need your mentee to know, understand, and be able to perform. In this case we are using "how to conduct a student–parent–teacher conference" as the skill to be developed.

Next, you will note a slightly larger circle that is labeled Level 1. A Level 1 experience is a vicarious experience that involves the mentee in a more limited capacity (e.g., observation, passive involvement, self-reflection) in which the goal is to become familiar and comfortable with the nature of the task or skill. Reading about the concept, watching a video, listening to a podcast, and talking to a more experienced other are all surface-level ways to acquire information about the "what and why" of what is needed to be learned.

In the example of how to facilitate a learning conference with students and parents, simply attending a series of meetings and watching the mentor in action is a great Level 1 experience. You can unpack the observation experience with your mentee and tease out the aspects (skills, ideas, components, etc.) that they noted. You can reinforce the policy or rationale for why the concept is important and its intended impact and purpose. So, a Level 1 experience is really a low-stress, low-risk opportunity for the mentee to see exemplary practice modeled for them.

Next comes Level 2. These are aspects of the learning task (concept) that the mentor now shifts to the mentee incrementally. In partnership with the mentor, the mentee begins to assume a measure of input or stake in the doing of the task. The key idea here is that the mentor creates an opportunity for the mentee to participate, contribute, or have some deliverable in conducting the task.

In this case, our mentee might have time in the conference to share observations of the student's progress for a given subject area or outcome. Speaking with parents and students in real time adds elements of healthy stress and rigor that a new teacher needs in speaking to the growth and development of the learner. We know that this can include some delicate or uncomfortable conversations, but this is where you as the mentor can guide, step in, or step back to allow the learning to unfold. In time, and in learning from missteps and mistakes, the mentee will gain more exposure to the concept and grow in their competency and confidence. Level 2 is a safe and trusting space where taking risks, trial and error, and learning from mistakes are encouraged by the mentor. This is why trust and respect are so important in the mentoring dynamic.

In time, we reach Level 3, which presses into the realm of mastery. This is the level where you, as mentor, should expect your mentee to take complete control and responsibility to consistently demonstrate success with the skill or concept. You should really be acting as a guide and serve as a support (a maintainer) as the mentee can now navigate their way through the learning task or skill independently. You are still available to debrief, bounce ideas, and support, but the true task for the mentor now is to challenge extensions of the learning into new areas.

In the case of the student conferences, Level 3 means the mentee is now fully capable of conducting the session on their own. They can navigate through challenging circumstances and know how and when to include school leaders. Furthermore, they are able to support peers and anticipate needs in advance. In essence, Level 3 means the mentee has the skills and tools to consistently do the given task well. When put together as noted in Figure 5.2, you can clearly see the increase of mentee responsibility and the decrease of mentor guidance as we move through the levels.

Figure 5.2 ◆ Levels of Experience Example

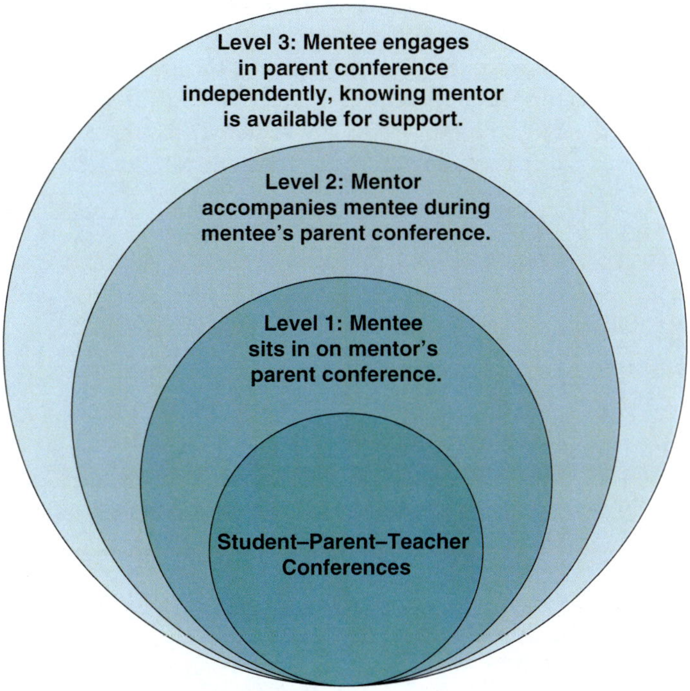

We know that some skills can be learned in a short period of time (taking attendance, morning routines, fire drill procedures, etc.). Some skills, like leading a student and parent learning meeting, can take months or a few years of practice and experience before the early career teacher reaches mastery. As a mentor, you need to know when to push in, press forward, ease back, and everything in between. Maintenance of the mentee's learning and progress will see changes in momentum. This is to be expected and again asks you as a mentor to know when to shift gears.

The Levels of Experience approach is one that we believe can help you to keep momentum going and allow you to become more of a maintainer as your mentee achieves mastery (or approaches mastery) in the many areas central to great teaching and learning. We invite you to explore more samples of how to develop skills with this model in Appendix B.

MENTORSHIP MOMENT

What are your thoughts on using the Levels of Experience Model with your mentee? Using the template provided in Appendix B (page 155), take some time to map out the three levels for a skill that you are currently working on with your mentee. Note: We have shared info and examples of the model (a Level 1 experience for you), and now we invite you to complete a template to demonstrate your understanding of the model (a Level 2 experience).

Mentorship Maintenance Moment #4: Feedback and Expert Noticing to Promote Mastery

Feedback is paramount to the success of any routine, and essential to the development of mastery in our aspiring leaders. We know that Level 2 experiences require a greater level or frequency of feedback whereas at Level 3 we would expect feedback only as required or to recalibrate a particular competency.

We will explore giving and receiving feedback in more depth in the next section, but because it's such a critical part of planning and guiding mastery experiences, we want to share some essential types of it now.

The Center for Creative Leadership (2024) outlines the four types of feedback that are most effective when communicating in a peer-to-peer or mentor-to-mentee relationship. See Figure 5.3 for their definitions of feedback.

Knowing these types of feedback helps us as mentor teachers be more intentional in helping our mentees learn. We offer the following approaches to feedback for your consideration:

Figure 5.3 ♦ The Most Effective Types of Feedback

1. **Actionable** feedback informs a person what they should be doing, even when phrased nicely. Example: *"I suggest you communicate more clearly when talking to your team via email."*

2. **Attributive** feedback describes a person's actions through labeling or through describing a personal quality. Example: *"You're an effective planner"; "You are very organized."*

3. **Contingency** feedback considers possible future consequences to direct current behavior. Example: *"If you don't leave time for students to think, they will never raise their hand to answer a question."*

4. **Impactful** feedback informs the receiver about the influence their actions have on people in their school or students in their classroom. This feedback expands on the "why" regarding behaviors that work or do not work. Example: *"The message you sent home to parents was confusing, which can lead to a feeling of frustration."*

Source: Adapted from Center for Creative Leadership. (2024)

GIVING AND RECEIVING FEEDBACK (EXPERT NOTICING)

Mentors who are skilled at providing feedback generally have a set of guiding parameters when it comes to the language they choose to apply. It is important to understand that feedback isn't simply what you choose to say; it's also important to consider how you deliver it to your mentee. Here are some common pitfalls, adapted from Center for Creative Leadership (2024), to avoid when engaging in the feedback process:

1. The feedback judges individuals, not actions.
2. The feedback is too vague.
3. The feedback speaks for others.
4. Negative feedback gets sandwiched between positive messages.
5. The feedback is exaggerated with generalities.
6. The feedback psychoanalyzes the motives behind behavior.
7. The feedback goes on too long.
8. The feedback contains an implied threat.
9. The feedback uses inappropriate humor.
10. The feedback is a question, not a statement.

As your mentee moves through the leveled experiences, it is important to determine when they may be ready to undertake a new challenge. Ideally, they will be ready when they exhibit elements of mastery. Ensuring our mentees are demonstrating mastery requires us to lean on our own personal expertise to seek out indications of success. Think about it in the context of the students you teach. When you have a rich understanding of your students and the learning outcomes the students are working toward, you can engage in an active process of interpretation of what you see in the learner. This is achieved in our classrooms by our use of "expert noticing."

This is how you determine the next course of action for your students:

1. Draw on your own content knowledge within the domain of new learning.
2. See the new learning from the perspective of your learners.
3. Recognize how the learners may approach the new content.

This is no different than what is required of mentors as they seek to identify mastery in their mentees. There need to be elements of expert noticing that are developed to ensure we are prepared to evaluate our mentees' progression toward mastery. When we as mentor teachers engage in the active process of attending to what is happening in a particular experience, and then interpret what they see according to the desired outcomes, we can be more deliberate in the preparation of our early career teachers. Remember, we want to know "the who before we do"!

ENGAGE IN EXPERT NOTICING

Engaging in expert noticing requires us to do all of the following:

1. Be selective and upfront about what we are seeking to identify.
2. Inform our mentee about the shared expectations for experiential learning.
3. Refine what we seek to notice to ensure we are developing a specific competency.
4. Look for successes as well as areas of improvement with our mentee.

Here is an example of these four phases of expert noticing in action. In being *selective and upfront* with her mentee, veteran elementary teacher Joy Singer is deliberate in her communication about what she is looking for. "When collaborating with my mentee, I remember to tell them not to sweat the big stuff. In fact," she shared, "we highlight small observable actions that both they and I feel need to be developed." By identifying the smaller actions taken by our mentees (*shared expectations for experiential learning*), we become more aware of what skills or concepts they need to address. For example, at the beginning of the school year, Joy invites her new mentee to join her at the classroom doorway to greet new students and their parents. "From this point, I am looking at how my mentee is welcoming students into our school environment and ensuring they are warm, inviting, and respectful. I also model expectations of morning routines and protocols." This highlights the significance of community and culture at school. When it comes to *refining and developing a specific competency*, Joy stated, "In thinking about the many tasks I need to work on with my mentee, it is important that I provide specific feedback in as timely a fashion as possible through multiple means." Joy and her mentee meet regularly to discuss what means of communication and feedback are most effective and helpful for growth and progress. "I value face-to-face meetings the most because we can engage in reflective conversation and chat about what I noticed versus what my mentee perceived." Joy also engages in a pre-meeting to set the expectations of the daily lessons and a post-meeting where both parties can have an open discussion about the experience. These actions speak to the importance of looking for successes as well as additional areas for growth. In cases where time does not permit face-to-face or pre- and post-meetings, an email or video chat can serve as a backup way to maintain the flow of feedback.

Finding what works best will require you to engage in these pre-conversations with your mentee to determine the type, frequency, and intensity of observations. Most importantly, your role and responsibility will be to notice areas of strength and areas for growth. Remember, the art of knowing when to push, pull, or let them fully take the wheel is truly at the heart of mentorship maintenance. Here are a few questions that can be used as you seek to notice the growth and needs of your mentee.

Reflection Questions for Expert Noticing

1. What am I noticing about my mentee as they engage in teaching tasks?
2. What does my mentee's level of engagement tell me about their current dispositions, unique characteristics, and needed learning opportunities?
3. How does my observation differ from that of my mentee's reflection on the experience?

Source: Adapted from Sherin et al. (2011).

Using these questions while maintaining the perspective of our mentees will afford us the opportunity to be evaluative without being judgmental as we seek to build mastery learning experiences. Naturally, it should be noted that exercising a feedback loop will be paramount to ensuring our mentees continue to feel supported as they realize greater self-efficacy and confidence in their teaching skills.

BUILDING TOWARD MASTERY

Expert noticing helps us to understand our impact as mentors. Clearly, we want our mentees to achieve success in all areas. We must maintain the expectation that all mentees want to be successful, that they can be successful, and that we will be able to guide them to that success. In fact, through building their confidence we are more likely to retain them in the profession. Once again, we are so thankful for your role in helping our early career teachers reach a high level of proficiency. As mentors, we must strive for rigor in the learning experiences we design, and keep an eye open for those sweet spots of complexity and challenge. The big question is this: How do you know when your mentee has reached a level of mastery? We offer Figure 5.4 as a visual that offers six "look fors" that will help you better determine when your mentee has attained mastery.

Figure 5.4 ◆ Things to Look For in Determining Mastery

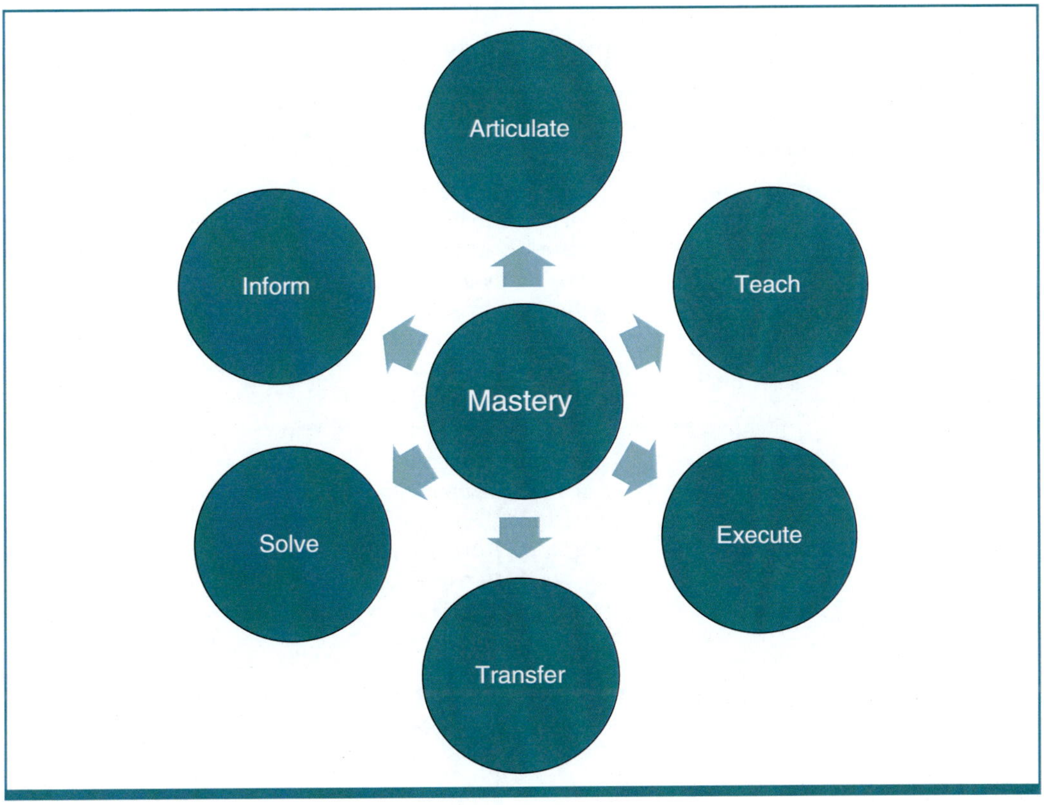

Here is a list of a few actions that you can notice not only in your growth as a mentor (ABCDs and T.I.M.E.) but more so in the growth and development of your mentee. Think of the following prompt: "I know I have attained a mastery level of understanding when . . ."

- I can *articulate* robust understanding of the concept criteria and *teach* it to others.
- I can consistently *execute* tasks effectively and efficiently (without my mentor's support).
- I am able to adapt and *transfer* concepts to new and different contexts (per Level 3).
- I can *solve* unique challenges and innovate new ways of doing things.
- I remain committed to *informing* my practice through lifelong learning.

Of course, these are not exhaustive examples; however, we do suggest keeping these action words handy to assist you in maintaining mentorship momentum day to day. Table 5.1 highlights some examples of what this may look like in practice.

TABLE 5.1 INQUIRY AREAS FOR NOTICING MASTERY

Focus of Mastery	Mentor Considerations	Ask Your Mentee
Articulate: Your mentee can clearly and confidently explain the nature of the skill or task.	This is beyond a Level 1 experience (basic or surface level) of understanding. You have confidence that the mentee understands the concept and content completely.	"Can you describe a specific instance where you felt confident in using this skill in the classroom? What elements contributed to that confidence?"
Teach: Your mentee can capably demonstrate (teach) the skill or task to their peers.	At Level 3 (mastery), your mentee can consistently, without assistance from you, demonstrate the skill or task to others. The mentee could support others at lower levels of experience (Level 1 or 2).	"In what ways can you assess and provide feedback on your progress in mastering this skill, and how would you support a colleague in their understanding of how to perform the skill?"

Focus of Mastery	Mentor Considerations	Ask Your Mentee
Execute: With fidelity to expected outcomes, the mentee can successfully perform the skill or task.	This includes the various subskills or subcomponents of the learning task that has been mastered by your mentee. Expect to observe consistency in the execution of the expected skill or task.	"What does mastery of this skill look like in action, and how might you plan to continually improve your execution of this skill?"
Transfer: The mentee can capably apply knowledge and ability inherent of the skill or task in new contexts or nuanced circumstances.	Your mentee is adept at responding to new scenarios by applying their skill and knowledge in varied or unexpected situations.	"How might you use your mastery of this skill in a new or challenging context, and how will you assess your ability to do so?"
Solve: The mentee is proactive in anticipating scenarios and leveraging knowledge and experience in addressing challenges.	Your mentee demonstrates a variety of approaches to addressing challenges and is proactive in leveraging available resources and advocating for others where needed.	"What specific problem-solving approaches do you find most effective, and how can you refine these methods in your teaching practice?"
Inform: The mentee is proactive in communicating their progress and apprising the mentor of how they are navigating both expected and unexpected tasks or situations.	Your mentee reaches out for matters requiring clarity or to leverage the mentor as a sounding board to explore ideas and solutions for more challenging matters that arise.	"In what ways can you seek feedback from me about your mastery of this skill, and how will you use that feedback to enhance your teaching practice?"

Through these six areas of inquiry, you can deepen the success of your expert noticing and triangulate the evidence of your mentee's growth and learning over time. It is our hope that the "tools" we have shared with you in this chapter will help you to feel prepared and be proactive when it comes to the "Zen and maintenance" of being an effective mentor. Let's wrap this chapter with a check-in on where you are at in terms of your ABCDs of being a mentorship maintainer.

UNPACKING OUR ABCDs OF MENTORSHIP MAINTENANCE

In Chapter 1, we spent some time addressing the importance of unpacking our *attitudes, biases, conceptual understanding,* and *dispositions* (ABCDs) toward mentorship. We offer two provocations for your reflection and consideration:

1. Having read this chapter on mentorship momentum, what are your ABCDs toward the need to maintain the relationship and dynamics of your mentorship pairing? Use the space provided to identify three ideas that have resonated most with you.

Idea 1.
Idea 2.
Idea 3.

2. With a colleague, share a *mentorship maintenance* idea from this chapter that you will commit to trying with your mentee.

Conclusion

If you look behind every exceptional person there is an exceptional teacher.

— Stephen Hawking (2018, p. 199)

THE MENTORSHIP MORAL IMPERATIVE

At the outset of this book, we presented the need to reframe and reclaim the many joys of what it means to be a teacher. Hawking's quote emphasizes the sentiment that the foundational role teachers play is shaping the future and enabling the success of human beings. Teachers provide the essential education and skills that empower individuals to pursue various careers.

We also pointed out, however, that, for a variety of reasons, we are having a difficult time not just attracting people into the profession but more so retaining them. Recall the staff room of 100 teachers we presented in the introduction where 55 of them will retire or leave the profession prematurely (Jotkoff, 2022; Walker, 2021); 33 are likely to leave teaching in the next two years (Will, 2023); 42 do not feel respected by the public (Gallup, 2024); 39 feel burned out (Gallup, 2024); and only 16 would recommend the profession of teaching to a young adult (Educators for Excellence, 2024). These statistics alone suggest that we face the moral imperative to not simply attract new teachers but do more to retain them. Thus, now more than ever, the mentorship of our early career teachers is our task at hand. It is what they are asking for!

Given the current challenges of teacher shortages, teacher burnout, lack of policy support, early retirements, difficult working conditions, and changing perceptions of the profession, we began this book with an appeal. We posted a "help wanted" sign, and we are so glad that you stepped up to offer your help. As a mentor teacher, you are perhaps the greatest resource and ally that K–12 systems have to help retain our new and early career teachers.

Our desire in writing this book was to provide you with resources, ideas, tips, tools, and approaches that would help to inform your *mentorship mindset*. Often, the mentorship of our early career teachers is left to chance or not fulsomely developed. Resources and supports for growing great mentors are not always readily available. We set out with this book to do more and help you to feel more capable and confident as a mentor to an early career teacher. It is our sincerest hope that our explorations of the Mentorship Mindset Model have, indeed, been of service and support to you, the teacher mentor we so greatly need. As we have said repeatedly, we need you and are deeply thankful that you have answered the call to serve as mentor to a new teacher. In answering the call, you are doing the following:

- **Supporting the Next Generation:** Mentoring helps cultivate the next generation of educators, ensuring they are well prepared and confident in their roles. This support can directly impact student learning and well-being.
- **Fostering Resilience:** By providing guidance and sharing experiences, mentor teachers can help new educators navigate challenges, reducing feelings of isolation and overwhelm. This support is crucial in combating burnout.
- **Building a Collaborative Culture:** Mentorship promotes a culture of collaboration and continuous learning

within schools, enhancing professional relationships and creating a more supportive work environment.

- **Upholding Standards of Excellence:** Experienced teachers can instill a sense of professionalism and commitment to high standards, ensuring that new teachers understand the importance of their role in shaping students' futures.
- **Addressing Equity and Inclusion:** Mentoring can focus on strategies for inclusive teaching, helping new teachers understand and meet the diverse needs of their students, which is essential for promoting equity in education.
- **Creating Sustainable Change:** By investing time and energy in mentoring, experienced teachers can help implement sustainable practices that improve the overall teaching environment and enhance job satisfaction for all educators.

In essence, as a teacher mentor, you are helping to reclaim and reframe the narrative of what it means to be a teacher today. In doing so, you are not only assisting in the growth and development of the very teachers our future generations of children need, but you are also creating the workplace conditions that will entice our early career teachers (and even more of you) to stay and be the difference in making our education systems stronger.

As we approach wrapping up our time together, we want to leave you with some final ideas and a mentorship self-awareness reflection tool that will help you to maintain your momentum and growth as a mentor teacher.

FINDING YOUR NORTH STAR

In Chapter 1, Vince talked about the use of a GPS to help find his way on a road trip in Alaska. A GPS makes finding our way very easy. Simply enter a destination, and ta-da, the system plots a route to reach the destination. Should unforeseen events happen (e.g., a road closure or accident), the GPS finds alternate ways to get there. It talks to us, providing guidance on what turns to make and lanes to take. Unfortunately, there is no GPS for mentoring another human being. More often than not, there is no road map. As mentors, we need to be able to find our way forward. We need to use a variety of means to plot our course.

As a naval officer, Tim reminds us that we need to use *all available means* to know where we are, where we need to be, and how to find the best way to get there. This means being attentive to the tools at our disposal when it comes to navigation. Visual bearings, a compass, radar, an echo sounder, radio waves, satellite systems, and stars can help us put a fix on the chart and know precisely where we are. As a watchkeeping officer, it is important to maintain a proper lookout to keep the ship and sailors safe. As a mentor, you too are a watchkeeper. You need to have a firm outlook of where your mentee needs to go (and grow). You will therefore need to make good use of the tools (such as the T.I.M.E. approaches) at your disposal (which again is the focus of this book). We want to help you find your way in helping your mentee find their way!

Since we mentioned stars, there is one in particular that helps navigators especially when the technology around us fails or is faulty. This star is Polaris, otherwise known as the North Star. It is constant in its position. It serves as an unwavering leadmark. A leadmark is a visible object (radio tower, lighthouse, church spire, prominent point of land, etc.) that we aim our efforts toward. If our ship is aiming at the leadmark, we can more easily determine if we are on track or being set off course. You must be the leadmark for your mentee. This means that you must be attuned to how you are finding your way as the mentor. To help you with this endeavor, we have provided a practical mentorship self-awareness tool in Table C.1 (page 142). Before we go there, let's first spend some time understanding what we mean by self-aware mentorship.

SELF-AWARE MENTORSHIP

Self-awareness consists of a range of components, which can be developed through focus, evaluation, and feedback, and provides an individual with an awareness of their inner state (emotions, cognitions, and physiological responses) that drives their behaviors (beliefs, values, and motivations) and an awareness of how this impacts and influences others. What does this mean for new teacher mentors? Being self-aware means we critically examine our own actions, decisions, and thought processes in understanding our influence and impact on the environments in which we live, work, and serve. Self-awareness calls us to assess our strengths and weaknesses via an honest examination of conscience. Self-identity, self-image, mindfulness, and metacognition are factors to consider in such an examination. This requires *making time* to reflect intentionally on our personal beliefs and values while being mindful of the vision and mission of the people and organization(s) we serve.

Why is self-awareness so important for you to consider as a mentor? We see mentors as leaders. As a self-reflective mentor, you must be willing to challenge personal assumptions and biases, especially unconscious and self-serving bias (recall your ABCDs). To be self-aware, you must embrace your tasks and challenges while welcoming disruptions to your thinking processes. Simply stated, you need the courage to invite critical feedback to inform your own metacognitive processes. Self-awareness is important because it builds discipline and fosters growth that helps you as a mentor to use your strengths to guide your mentee to the best possible outcomes. Let's face it: As human beings, we sometimes default to "this is how I have always done things." The danger of this is we often take our daily disposition toward mentorship for granted. We become closed to possibilities about how to be more versatile, flexible, or efficacious in serving those we lead. Through being self-aware we seek to understand our feelings and attitudes not only about the *why* and *what* we must do but more so about *how* we will do it! What, then, is an effective way to become a more self-aware mentor?

For us, self-awareness means being attuned to our disposition to serve others. This means that we must have both contextual and situational awareness of the needs of others. This requires having a rich sense of their affective state and, equally important, our own. Bandura (1977) reminds us that our affective state is how we feel about our own capabilities and capacity to organize actions and navigate challenges: "People with high assurance in their capabilities approach difficult tasks as challenges to be mastered rather than as threats to be avoided" (p. 11). In terms of being self-aware, a mentor needs to understand how to be assured in times of adversity versus succumbing to avoidance of challenges. Self-wellness, which we suggest is an integral part of self-awareness, is key to achieving this.

Let's think about self-wellness this way. When conducting preflight safety checks, an airline attendant reminds us that we must first know how to put on our own oxygen mask before helping others. This always sounds counterintuitive in a leader's mind. Why? We are so used to doing for others first that we often forget self-care. To be self-aware as a mentor, we must be at peace with knowing how we feel and what we need to be best oriented to the mentorship (leadership) we provide each day.

How do I (Tim) go about determining my positionality toward my own mentorship self-awareness? I contemplate the challenges and joys ahead of me each day so that I can be best equipped to navigate my day. I use a reflective "self check-in" that enables me to assess my daily disposition to serving the people I work with. I consider internal and external factors to gauge how I might best respond to the needs of my students, staff, and other stakeholders.

Think about the airline attendant again and the preflight safety checks that must be done in advance of takeoff. Knowing the state of the team and equipment, verifying that required resources are readily on hand, and conducting a scan of environmental factors form a considerable part of being attenuated to the work to be done. It is necessary for the leader to be self-aware as to how to best *prepare for* and *engage with* the tasks of the day.

A SELF-AWARENESS TOOL FOR TEACHER MENTORS

While there are many processes and self-check tools available to leaders, we are practitioners of a check-in (Cusack, 2023) that helps to center four factors of the mentor's self: *head, heart, hands, and heels*. We detail these in Table C.1.

TABLE C.1 FOUR-FACTOR SELF-AWARENESS TOOL

Factor	What I consider	Questions I ask myself
Head (cognitive dispositions) Think about what the day will bring (planned or otherwise) and how to prepare mentally for my mentorship today.	• The tasks I am called to do • My priorities for work, home, and self • What is important to achieve today	• Am I organized for what I know needs to happen today? • What tools and resources will be helpful to achieve my goals today? • What strategies might help me realize greater focus and success today?

Factor	What I consider	Questions I ask myself
Heart (affective dispositions) Think about the relationships I need to nurture or manage. Understand how I feel (self-care) and how my affect might impact the well-being of others.	• How I feel about the tasks I must do today • What excites me • What worries me • Who needs more (or less) of my time and attention	• Do I need to give myself a pep talk? • Do I need someone else to give me a pep talk? • Who needs my care, focus, time, or attention today?
Hands (orientation to actions) Think about how I will action (do or fulfill) the tasks and demands of the day.	• Who needs hands-on help or support • What needs to speed up or slow down • What needs building up vs. tearing down	• Who needs a pat on the back? • Who requires a soft (or firm) touch for a difficult problem? • Who needs to be embraced or waved off? • What do I need to hold on to (or let go of)?
Heels (commitment to actions) Think about a mentor's resolve, resiliency, and commitment to actions. Walk the talk of *head*, *heart*, and *hands*.	• How I will move toward what needs to be done (at a full sprint, with my heels dug in, at a slower pace, or by stepping back a bit) • Any delicate dances needed to navigate obstacles	• What pace must I consider to achieve specific tasks? • Am I running toward or away from a problem that I really need to address? • Do I need to walk alongside, in front, or behind to best support my team?

Adapted from Cusack, T. P. (2023, May 7). How to become a self-aware school leader. *Education Week*. https://www.edweek.org/leadership/opinion-how-to-become-a-self-aware-school-leader/2023/05

Self-awareness is an essential process to personal growth and development as a mentor. It requires a willingness to be vulnerable and honest with ourselves about our strengths and weaknesses. Self-awareness involves examining situations from different perspectives and considering the impact of our affect and actions on others. Through an examination of internal and external factors using a self-reflective process, we can attenuate ourselves more capably and robustly (*head, heart, hands,* and *heels*) to understanding how to best embrace and engage with the challenges and joys we encounter daily in serving the needs of our mentees and, ultimately, thriving within our respective learning communities.

Being a self-aware mentor means understanding your strengths, weaknesses, biases, and emotions, as well as the impact you have on others. It's about being mindful of your actions, your words, and the way you guide your mentees. Here's what being a self-aware mentor involves:

1. **Understanding Your Own Values and Beliefs:** Recognize what drives you and how your values shape your mentoring style. This awareness helps ensure you're guiding mentees based on their needs, not just your perspectives.
2. **Recognizing Biases:** Be aware of any conscious or unconscious biases that could affect your judgment. This means being mindful of how you respond to different mentees and ensuring fairness in your guidance.
3. **Emotional Intelligence:** Self-aware mentors can manage their emotions and respond thoughtfully rather than reactively. They understand how their emotional state can affect their mentees and adjust accordingly.
4. **Seeking Feedback:** Self-aware mentors are open to feedback from their mentees and others. They view feedback as a tool for growth, not criticism, and use it to refine their mentoring approach.
5. **Reflective Practice:** Regularly reflecting on your mentoring experiences helps you identify areas for improvement. This could include evaluating what went well in a mentoring session and what could have been handled differently.
6. **Setting Boundaries:** Knowing your limits and setting clear boundaries with mentees ensures a healthy, respectful relationship. This self-awareness prevents overstepping and maintains professionalism.
7. **Authenticity:** Self-aware mentors are genuine and honest. They acknowledge when they don't know something and are willing to learn alongside their mentees.
8. **Empathy and Understanding:** Being self-aware means recognizing how your actions and words affect others. A self-aware mentor listens actively and strives to understand their mentee's perspective.

Overall, self-awareness in mentoring fosters a more effective, empathetic, and adaptive relationship, benefiting both the mentor and the mentee. Our hope is that you will take time to look after your health and well-being. In doing so, you allow more time, space, and grace to be the best mentor you can be for your mentee.

FINAL WORDS ON THE MENTORSHIP MINDSET

From our ABCDs of mentorship, T.I.M.E approaches, and mentorship matching to our momentum-building and mentorship maintenance ideas, we genuinely hope you feel more equipped to serve as a mentor. In reclaiming and reframing the narrative of what it means to be a teacher today, we hope that you will be among the *9 in 10 teachers* who we want to promote the profession. Through the dedicated work of your hands and heels, we sincerely thank you for the head work and, above all, the heart work that you invest in your mentee. Our children and their children will forever be thankful that you answered that "help wanted" sign and stepped up to serve as a great mentor to an early career teacher.

Thank you!

Vince, Tim, and Wayne

APPENDIX A

Mentorship Modality Inventory

To what extent do you agree with each statement and its corresponding impact on creating effective mentorship? This inventory will provide you with a series of statements about mentoring. We invite you to read each statement and indicate the extent the statement resonates with you (e.g., the extent to which you agree or disagree). Be sure to respond to all the statements and answer based on your personal understanding and experience.

SCORING: 1 = *totally disagree*, 2 = *somewhat disagree*, 3 = *neither agree nor disagree*, 4 = *somewhat agree*, 5 = *totally agree*

1.	Mentorship is best viewed as a form of apprenticeship with the mentor serving as the experienced master.	1	2	3	4	5
2.	Hands-on (practical) real-world experiences provide the most effective way to develop a mentee's skills.	1	2	3	4	5
3.	Stimulating critical thinking skills through good questioning techniques is necessary for successful mentoring.	1	2	3	4	5

4.	Developing trust is the most important aspect of successful mentorship.	1	2	3	4	5
5.	To be effective, mentoring should take place over a longer period of time.	1	2	3	4	5
6.	Good mentoring should see both the mentor and mentee learning from (and with) each other.	1	2	3	4	5
7.	There needs to be opportunity for the mentee to teach or exchange knowledge with the mentor.	1	2	3	4	5
8.	Ideally there should be a generational difference (gap) between mentor and mentee.	1	2	3	4	5
9.	Mentoring should include knowledge sharing from multiple perspectives.	1	2	3	4	5
10.	Regular feedback cycles focused on goal setting is a good way to foster continuous learning for a mentee.	1	2	3	4	5
11.	The mentor and mentee should collaborate on setting realistic and attainable goals.	1	2	3	4	5
12.	Mentors should teach the mentee specific cognitive strategies to promote problem solving, critical thinking, and knowledge recall.	1	2	3	4	5
13.	To be effective, any feedback must "feed forward" to improve future learning outcomes.	1	2	3	4	5
14.	It is important that ample time be given to focus on metacognition, problem-solving skills, and the application of knowledge.	1	2	3	4	5
15.	Mentorship must leverage self-inquiry, awareness of thought processes, and self-directed learning.	1	2	3	4	5
16.	Mentorship must include elements of cultural awareness, diversity, and inclusion training.	1	2	3	4	5
17.	Opportunities for the mentor and mentee to engage in cross-cultural experiences are important for promoting deeper understanding of each other's backgrounds.	1	2	3	4	5
18.	The sharing of cultural narratives (storytelling) is a key part of successful mentorship.	1	2	3	4	5
19.	Human connection, creating a sense of belonging, and breaking down stereotypes are essential to effective mentorship.	1	2	3	4	5
20.	To be effective, mentoring pairings should seek like-minded individuals with similar cultural backgrounds and beliefs.	1	2	3	4	5

DETERMINING YOUR PREFERRED MENTORSHIP MODALITY

- Add your scores for Questions 1–5. These are considered *traditional* approaches to mentoring.
- Add your scores for Questions 6–10. These are considered *interdependent* approaches to mentoring.
- Add your scores for Questions 11–15. These are considered *metacognitive* approaches to mentoring.
- Add your scores for Questions 16–20. These are considered *environmental* (learning culture) approaches to mentoring.

In the space provided, list your score for each of the four areas:

Mentorship Modality	Score
Traditional (Questions 1–5)	
Interdependent (Questions 6–10)	
Metacognitive (Questions 11–15)	
Environmental (Questions 16–20)	

A LITTLE MORE TIME FOR T.I.M.E.

Mentoring new teachers is an essential strategy for developing their skills, promoting retention, and ensuring long-term success in the classroom. In Chapter 2, we helped you to learn more about your "default" mentorship style through use of our T.I.M.E. approaches. We showed you four domains: *traditional, interdependent, metacognitive,* and *environmental*. For each domain, we provide further examples and research to highlight the effectiveness of these strategies.

I Traditional (T)

Traditional mentoring styles involve methods where mentors often take a more directive or expert role in guiding and teaching new educators. These styles provide a clear framework of instruction and feedback to help new teachers develop their craft.

a. **Direct Instruction and Modeling**
   - Approach: Mentors demonstrate effective teaching strategies, modeling lessons or classroom management techniques while the mentee observes. The mentor then provides feedback and suggestions for improvement.
   - Example: Mentors may model specific instructional strategies like questioning techniques or differentiated instruction, followed by collaborative discussions.
   - Research:
     - Kraft et al. (2018) found that direct observation and modeling of best practices by mentors have a significant impact on new teachers' instructional quality and student achievement.

b. **Coteaching**
   - Approach: Mentors and mentees coteach lessons to allow the mentee to learn by doing while receiving real-time guidance and support from the mentor.
   - Example: New teachers gradually take on more responsibility in teaching while the mentor provides support in areas such as pacing, content delivery, or student engagement.
   - Research:
     - Cornett and Knight (2009) found that coteaching fosters a supportive environment for new teachers and accelerates their learning by providing immediate feedback and shared responsibility.

c. **Feedback and Reflection**
   - Approach: After each lesson, mentors give constructive feedback on what went well and areas to improve, focusing on specific aspects such as student engagement or lesson clarity.
   - Example: In structured feedback sessions, mentors provide feedback based on preestablished goals and observations.
   - Research:
     - Hunzicker (2017) highlights that structured feedback after classroom observations helps new teachers understand their strengths and areas for growth, fostering professional development.

2 Interdependent (I)

Interdependent mentoring styles emphasize collaboration and mutual learning between the mentor and the mentee. These approaches focus on shared responsibility for growth and involve both the mentor and the mentee in learning from one another.

a. **Peer Coaching**
   - Approach: New teachers and experienced teachers observe each other, discuss teaching strategies, and provide constructive feedback in a reciprocal manner.
   - Example: A peer mentor observes a new teacher's lesson and provides feedback, while also receiving feedback from the new teacher on their own practices.
   - Research:
     - Rodgers et al. (2018) found that peer coaching supports new teachers by promoting collaborative learning and increasing confidence, with both parties benefiting from shared expertise.

b. **Collaborative Lesson Planning**
   - Approach: Mentors and mentees work together to design and plan lessons, sharing resources and strategies and making decisions collectively to enhance the learning experience.
   - Example: A mentor and mentee collaboratively plan a series of lessons, with the mentor suggesting adjustments based on experience and the mentee bringing in innovative ideas.
   - Research:
     - Long et al. (2016) argue that collaborative lesson planning improves teaching quality and promotes professional growth by drawing on the strengths and ideas of both teachers.

c. **Group Mentoring and Professional Learning Communities**
   - Approach: In group mentoring or professional learning communities (PLCs), new teachers meet regularly with a mentor or coach, as well as other new or experienced teachers, to discuss challenges, share best practices, and engage in professional development activities.
   - Example: New teachers participate in regular PLC meetings to discuss strategies, review student data, and receive feedback on instructional practices.
   - Research:
     - Darling-Hammond et al. (2019) support the idea that PLCs promote teacher collaboration and improve teaching outcomes by fostering interdependent relationships and collective problem solving.

3 Metacognitive (M)

Metacognitive mentoring involves strategies that encourage new teachers to think critically about their own practice, fostering self-awareness and reflective thinking. These approaches focus on helping teachers develop their own solutions to challenges through self-reflection and problem solving.

a. **Reflective Journals**
    - Approach: Teachers maintain journals to reflect on their teaching experiences, identifying challenges, successes, and strategies they plan to use in the future.
    - Example: Mentors encourage new teachers to write reflective journals after each lesson, providing a space for self-examination and deeper understanding of their teaching practices.
    - Research:
        - Schön (2017) emphasizes that reflective journaling helps teachers internalize lessons from practice and develop critical thinking skills that lead to improved instructional decisions.

b. **Guided Self-Reflection**
    - Approach: Mentors guide new teachers through structured self-reflection, using open-ended questions to help them critically examine their teaching practices.
    - Example: After a lesson, the mentor might ask reflective questions: "What worked well today? What would you do differently next time? How did your students respond?"
    - Research:
        - Costa and Garmston (2015) demonstrate that reflective questioning helps new teachers become more aware of their teaching decisions and develop strategies for improvement.

c. **Goal Setting and Self-Monitoring**
    - Approach: New teachers set specific, measurable goals for improving their teaching, which they track and reflect on throughout the school year.
    - Example: A mentor and new teacher might collaboratively set goals related to classroom management or student engagement, with the new teacher self-monitoring progress and revising strategies.
    - Research:
        - Hunzicker (2017) discusses how goal setting enhances teacher efficacy and provides a road map for new teachers to develop their skills through systematic self-reflection.

4 Environmental (E)

Environmental (and cultural) factors refer to the context in which teaching takes place, including the school climate, cultural norms, and community dynamics. Effective mentorship takes these factors into account to support new teachers' adaptation to their school environment.

a. **Culturally Responsive Teaching Practices** (see Appendix B for more)
   - Approach: Mentors help new teachers integrate culturally relevant teaching strategies that acknowledge and value the diverse backgrounds of students.
   - Example: Mentors provide guidance on how to incorporate students' cultural contexts into lesson planning, promoting inclusivity and student engagement.
   - Research:
     - Gay (2018) emphasizes that culturally responsive teaching is crucial for fostering an inclusive classroom environment, and mentors play a vital role in supporting new teachers in this practice.

b. **Social-Emotional Support and Community Building**
   - Approach: Mentors help new teachers navigate the emotional and social aspects of teaching, particularly the stress and isolation that can come with being a novice teacher.
   - Example: Mentors encourage new teachers to build positive relationships with students, colleagues, and families, creating a supportive network.
   - Research:
     - Gimbert et al. (2023) found that social-emotional support from mentors helps reduce stress and burnout in new teachers, likely contributing to improved retention rates and greater job satisfaction.

c. **School Culture Orientation**
   - Approach: Mentors help new teachers understand and adapt to the specific norms, values, and expectations of their school or district, ensuring that they feel integrated into the school community.
   - Example: A mentor might guide a new teacher through understanding school policies, navigating faculty meetings, and aligning with the school's mission and vision.
   - Research:
     - Coggshall et al. (2021) highlight that helping new teachers adjust to the school culture through

mentorship can improve their effectiveness and retention, especially in schools with high expectations and strong community values.

CONCLUSION

The four T.I.M.E. domains—traditional, interdependent, metacognitive, and environmental—provide a comprehensive framework for mentoring new teachers. Research shows that combining direct teaching strategies with opportunities for self-reflection, collaborative learning, and cultural adaptation significantly enhances the effectiveness of mentorship programs. By incorporating these diverse strategies, you, as a mentor, can help new teachers grow in their craft, adapt to their teaching environment, and thrive in their professional development.

APPENDIX B

Levels of Experience: Theory Into Practice

In Chapter 5, we described our "leveling up" model (see Figure 5.1, page 125). It is an approach that helps you, as the mentor, guide your mentee from a surface level of understanding of a desired skill (Level 1), to a deeper level of understanding and application of the skill (Level 2), to the ultimate goal of reaching a level of mastery (Level 3) whereby the mentee can apply or extend the skill to different, more complex, or emerging contexts.

We wish to provide you with a further illustration of what this might look like. Following the examples in Figures B.1 and B.2, you will find a blank Levels of Experience template for your use. We encourage you to work with your mentee in identifying a particular skill, concept, or competency to develop and use the model to inform your thinking and planning in terms of the activities and experiences required to move from Level 1 to Level 3.

Scenario: Your mentee is struggling with some aspects of classroom management. More precisely, the students call out at random, they do not fully engage in listening when the teacher is providing direct instruction, and there are increasing levels of disruption in corners of the room. While classroom management comprises many necessary skills and competencies, your conversations with the mentee suggest that they really want to work on classroom communication protocols that might help with better student engagement. You consider your own practices and then suggest that the mentee focus on some effective questioning techniques. Using the handy Levels of Experience template, you map out the following guided learning experiences for your mentee.

Level 1 asks us to consider the sources and resources that will help us to understand the competency, concept, or skill (area of inquiry) to be developed. In the case of Figure B.1, we want to find information on what are known to be effective questioning techniques to better promote student participation and engagement. Level 2 invites you as the mentor to model the area of inquiry and then have the mentee try. This is a safe

Figure B.1 ◆ Effective Questioning Techniques

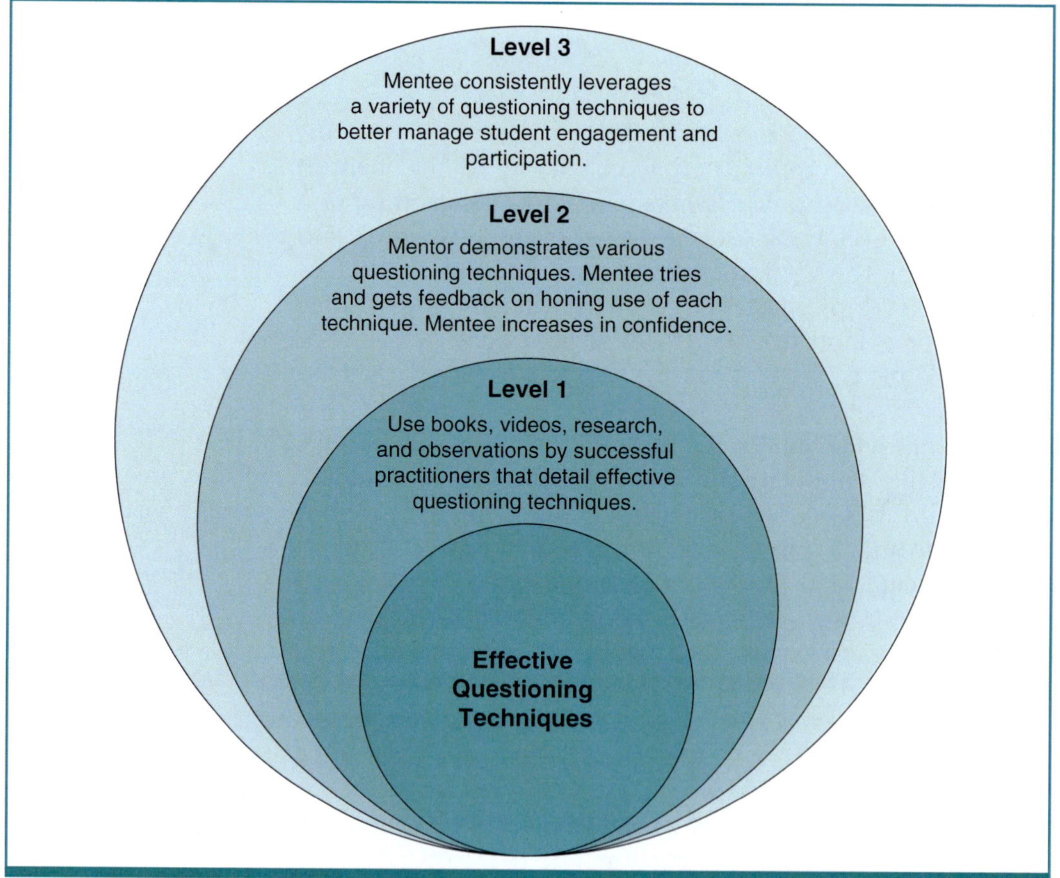

playground where your mentee can take risks, make mistakes, try and try again, and keep working toward honing the skill. Level 2 is likely where you will be most hands-on in terms of offering feedback and encouragement, especially in the earlier iterations of the use of the questioning techniques. Signs of success will be improvement in student attentiveness and responsiveness to your mentee. In Level 3, you will step back to a great degree as your mentee consistently and capably demonstrates the area of inquiry to great effect (ideally a level of mastery). Your role now is to offer insights on how to further extend or deepen the application of the skill(s).

We wish to note that whereas our example of effective questioning techniques is only one aspect of how a new teacher can experience greater success with classroom management, the model can be used to drill deeper into one specific technique at a time. In our complementary book, *Navigating the First Years: A Toolkit for Classroom Success* (Bustamante et al., in press), we offer a detailed section on effective questioning techniques that move beyond basic W5 + H style (Toolbox Tactic 5.6: Developing Your Questioning Techniques [The Art of Questioning]). One of them is called Live Auction, and another is called Echo.

How to Use Live Auction: Ask students a question—for example, "Who can tell me one important aspect of photosynthesis?" Pause for two seconds and then go into auctioneer mode. Ask, "Who wishes to answer? Raise your hand." As hands go up, simply count them out loud: "I see one hand. Do I have two? I have two hands. Is there a third? Oh, I see four! Can I have five? I see five hands. How about six?" (And so on). Essentially, try to get as many hands as possible, and then pick a student to respond. This gives you a quick check as to which students feel confident to respond. Students like the fun of the fast-paced counting of hands. Once you get an answer, move to the Echo technique.

How to Use Echo: As soon as a student answers a question correctly, go to three or four students around the room and simply ask them to repeat (echo) what was said. This reinforces the concept (not just correct answer) and allows students who normally might not raise their hand (as in the Live Auction technique) to repeat a correct answer. This is a low-stakes way to encourage the participation of reluctant students and also keeps all students on their toes for listening to their peers. By offering praise—a simple "thank you"—as you move on to the next student to echo the same answer, you increase motivation and impart a sense of participation in the reluctant student.

Using the Levels of Experience Model (Figure 5.1, page 125), let's detail what a plan would look like to implement your mentee's use of the Live Auction and Echo techniques in addressing their desire to improve communication protocols and student engagement through effective questioning techniques (see Figure B.2).

Things to remember: Some skills can be moved from Level 1 to Level 3 in a short period of time. Many skills, however, take a greater amount of time. As a mentor, it is important to communicate frequently with your mentee to understand how they are feeling about their progress from level to level and to know when to push, pull, or ease off a bit to help your mentee move forward. Be patient. Be persistent. Celebrate each small victory!

Figure B.2 • Live Auction and Echo Techniques

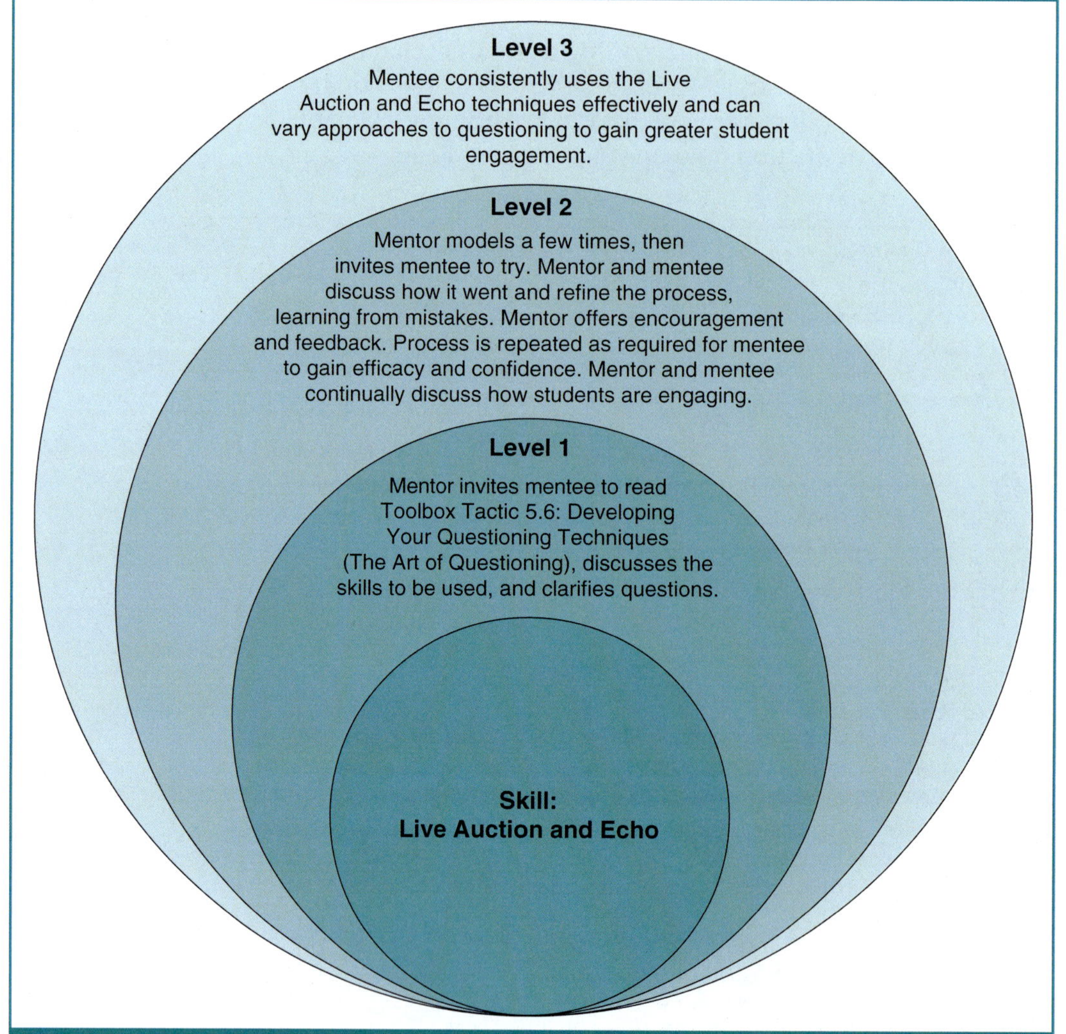

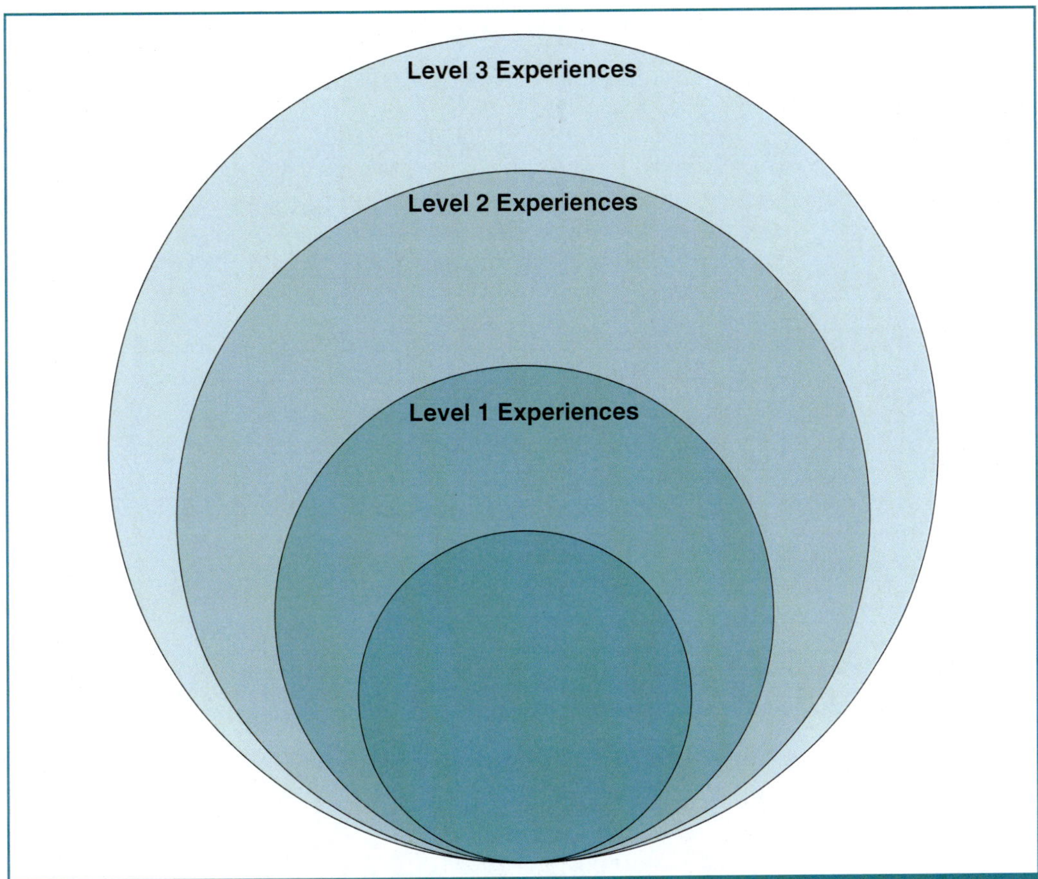
Level 3 Experiences
Level 2 Experiences
Level 1 Experiences

APPENDIX C

A Shoutout to Coaching

We would be remiss in a book about mentoring not to reinforce the important role that coaching has in mentorship processes. While we teased out differences between coaching and mentoring in Chapter 1, we know that coaching is a highly effective method for helping new teachers develop their skills, gain confidence, and improve their practice. Over the past several years, numerous coaching methods and strategies have been identified as effective in supporting novice educators. We note that you as a mentor will likely leverage many coaching techniques and strategies in working with your mentee, but you may also need to outsource (bring in other experts) to help in areas that may not necessarily be in your area of expertise. Here are some well-known coaching methods and strategies that have been shown to be effective in preparing early career teachers.

1. **Instructional Coaching**
   - Overview: Instructional coaching involves a coach working directly with teachers to improve their instructional practices. This method is focused on specific teaching strategies and often involves modeling, observation, feedback, and collaborative planning.

- Effective Strategies:
  - Modeling and Coteaching: Coaches may model effective lessons or coteach with the mentee, allowing for direct observation and collaboration.
  - Focused Observation: Coaches observe specific areas of practice (e.g., classroom management, questioning techniques) and provide feedback based on these observations.
- Research:
  - Kraft et al. (2018) found that instructional coaching significantly improves teachers' instructional practices and student achievement, particularly when coaches are highly skilled and the coaching is sustained over time.
  - Cornett and Knight (2009) discuss how instructional coaching enhances teacher effectiveness by providing personalized, in-the-moment feedback and support tailored to the teacher's needs.

2. **Cognitive Coaching**
   - Overview: Cognitive coaching focuses on developing the cognitive skills of teachers, encouraging them to reflect on their teaching practices and make decisions that promote student learning. The coach helps the teacher gain insight into their own teaching through reflective questioning and dialogue.
   - Effective Strategies:
     - Reflective Questioning: Coaches use open-ended questions to help the teacher reflect on their practice and identify areas for improvement.
     - Goal Setting and Self-Monitoring: Coaches work with teachers to set specific, measurable goals and help them monitor progress over time.
   - Research:
     - Costa and Garmston (2015) emphasize that cognitive coaching develops teachers' reflective thinking and problem-solving skills, leading to greater autonomy and improved teaching practices.
     - Hunzicker (2017) highlights that cognitive coaching fosters a collaborative relationship between the coach and teacher, which can lead to increased teacher efficacy and sustained growth.
3. **Peer Coaching**
   - Overview: Peer coaching involves teachers coaching one another. Teachers work together to observe and provide feedback, share strategies, and engage in

mutual professional development. This collaborative approach fosters a sense of community and support.

- Effective Strategies:
  - Lesson Study: Teachers collaboratively plan, teach, and then observe each other's lessons, providing feedback on strategies, student engagement, and lesson design.
  - Feedback Loops: Peer coaches exchange feedback after lessons or teaching sessions, with a focus on specific aspects of instruction such as questioning techniques, classroom management, or differentiation.
- Research:
  - Long et al. (2016) found that peer coaching, especially when teachers focus on specific teaching techniques and engage in ongoing feedback, can lead to significant improvements in teaching practices.
  - Rodgers et al. (2018) demonstrated that peer coaching fosters professional growth through collaboration, encourages reflective practice, and increases teacher confidence.

4. **Video-Based Coaching**
   - Overview: Video-based coaching allows teachers to record their lessons and then work with a coach to analyze the footage. This approach provides teachers with a clear view of their teaching practices and allows for detailed reflection and feedback.
   - Effective Strategies:
     - Self-Reflection: Teachers review their videos and reflect on their instructional strategies, classroom management, and student engagement before meeting with the coach for feedback.
     - Targeted Feedback: Coaches and teachers use video to pinpoint specific areas for improvement and then collaboratively develop action plans.
   - Research:
     - Video coaching enhances teachers' ability to reflect on their practice by offering them an opportunity to critically analyze and improve specific aspects of teaching (van Es et al., 2015).
     - van der Linden et al. (2022) suggest video-based coaching is effective in helping teachers improve their classroom management skills and lesson delivery by allowing them to observe and self-assess their teaching.

5. **The Gradual Release of Responsibility Model**
   - Overview: This strategy is based on the idea that new teachers gradually take on more responsibility for their teaching with the coach's support. The coach initially models teaching practices, then moves to joint teaching, followed by independent practice.
   - Effective Strategies:
     - Modeling to Collaboration: The coach initially models the teaching practice, then the coach and teacher collaborate, and eventually the teacher independently applies the strategies learned.
     - Scaffolded Support: Coaches provide varying levels of support depending on the teacher's readiness and confidence, gradually reducing assistance as the teacher becomes more proficient.
   - Research:
     - Ben-Anram and Davidovitch (2024) argue that the gradual release model is a highly effective method for supporting novice teachers as they transition from being observers to independent practitioners.
     - Shank and Santiague (2021) (asserted that this method helps build teacher capacity by giving them a structured pathway for development while fostering a sense of autonomy.
6. **The Collaborative Coaching Model**
   - Overview: This model emphasizes the partnership between the coach and the teacher, where both work together as equal partners in the development process. It is based on the idea that teachers are experts in their own practice and the coach supports them in refining and enhancing their skills.
   - Effective Strategies:
     - Coplanning and Coteaching: Coaches and teachers coplan lessons and coteach, with the coach providing guidance and feedback during the process.
     - Shared Reflection: After lessons, the coach and teacher engage in reflective conversations about what went well and areas for improvement.
   - Research:
     - Knight (2019) highlights that collaborative coaching builds trust and mutual respect, creating an environment where teachers feel comfortable experimenting with new strategies and receiving feedback.
     - Darling-Hammond et al. (2019) emphasize that collaborative coaching is linked to improved

teaching practices and increased teacher retention, particularly when the coaching is sustained and embedded in school culture.

7. **Data-Driven Coaching**
   - Overview: This method involves using student data (e.g., assessments, surveys) to inform coaching decisions. Coaches and teachers work together to analyze the data and make adjustments to instructional strategies based on student performance.
   - Effective Strategies:
     - Student Performance Analysis: Coaches help teachers analyze student work and assessment data to identify patterns and areas where teaching methods can be improved.
     - Goal Setting Based on Data: Teachers set specific, data-informed goals for improving student outcomes, which the coach helps them achieve.
   - Research:
     - Saunders et al. (2024) found that using data in coaching conversations provides concrete evidence for making instructional adjustments, leading to improvements and implementation of evidence-informed practices in both teaching and student learning outcomes.
     - Reddy et al. (2021) highlight the role of data-driven coaching in improving teacher practice by focusing on student performance data to inform instructional changes.

CONCLUSION

Coaching has become an essential method for professional development, particularly for new teachers. Effective coaching methods, such as instructional coaching, cognitive coaching, and peer coaching, all contribute to developing teachers' skills, promoting self-reflection, and improving student outcomes. Research continues to support the effectiveness of these methods, showing that personalized coaching, when tailored to the individual needs of teachers and integrated with real-time feedback, can lead to substantial improvements in both teaching practices and student achievement.

References

A-ha. (1985). Take on me [Song]. *On Hunting high and low*. Warner Bros. Records.

Bandura, A. (1977). Self-efficacy: Toward a unifying theory of behavioral change. *Psychological Review, 84*(2), 191–215. https://doi.org/10.1037/0033-295X.84.2.191

Bandura, A. (1989). Human agency in social cognitive theory. *American Psychologist, 44*(9), 1175–1184. https://doi.org/10.1037/0003-066X.44.9.1175

Ben-Amram, M., & Davidovitch, N. (2024). Novice teachers and mentor teachers: From a traditional model to a holistic mentoring model in the postmodern era. *Education Sciences, 14*(2), 143.

Brendtro, L. K., Brokenleg, M., & Van Bockern, S. (2019). *Reclaiming youth at risk: Futures of promise* (3rd ed.). Solution Tree Press.

Bustamante, V., Adomako-Ansah, S., Cusack, T. P., & Davies, W. (in press). *Navigating the first years: A toolkit for classroom success*. Corwin.

Callahan, J. (2016). Encouraging retention of new teachers through mentoring strategies. *Delta Kappa Gamma Bulletin, 83*(1), 6.

Center for Creative Leadership. (2024, September 27). *How to give feedback most effectively*. https://www.ccl.org/articles/leading-effectively-articles/review-time-how-to-give-different-types-of-feedback/

Chesley, G. M., & Jordan, J. (2012). What's missing from teacher prep. *Educational Leadership, 69*(8), 41–45. https://www.learntechlib.org/p/91047/

Coggshall, J., Davidson-Gibbs, D., & Wayne, A. (2021). *Measuring the fidelity of implementation of instructional coaching: Current approaches and new directions*. Society for Research on Educational Effectiveness.

Cornett, J., & Knight, J. (2009). Research on coaching. In J. Knight (Ed.), *Coaching: Approaches and perspectives* (pp. 192–216). Corwin.

Costa, A. L., & Garmston, R. J. (2015). *Cognitive coaching: Developing self-directed leaders and learners*. Rowman & Littlefield.

Curtis, E., Martin, R., & Broadley, T. (2019). Reviewing the purpose of professional experience: A case study in initial teacher education reform. *Teaching and Teacher Education, 83*, 77–86. https://doi.org/10.1016/j.tate.2019.03.017

Cusack, T. P. (2023, May 7). How to become a self-aware school leader. *Education Week*. https://www.edweek.org/leadership/opinion-how-to-become-a-self-aware-school-leader/2023/05

Cusack, T., & Bustamante, V. (2023). *Leader ready: Four pathways to prepare aspiring school leaders*. Corwin.

Darling-Hammond, L., Chung, R., & Frelow, F. (2002). Variation in teacher preparation: How well do different pathways prepare teachers to teach? *Journal of Teacher Education, 53*(4), 286–302. https://doi-org.proxy1.lib.uwo.ca/10.1177/0022487102053004002

Darling-Hammond, L., Saunders, R., Podolsky, A., Kini, T., Espinoza, D., Hyler, M., & Carver-Thomas, D. (2019). *Best practices to recruit and retain well-prepared teachers in all classrooms*. Learning Policy Institute.

Educators for Excellence. (2024). *Voices from the classroom: A survey of America's educators*. https://e4e.org/wp-content/uploads/2024/05/2024-Voices-from-the-Classroom-Report.pdf

Gallup. (2024). *The state of schools report: Insights to inform higher education and K–12 leaders*. https://www.gallup.com/education/608843/state-of-schools-report-2024.aspx

Gay, G. (2018). *Culturally responsive teaching: Theory, research, and practice*. Teachers College Press.

Gimbert, B. G., Miller, D., Herman, E., Breedlove, M., & Molina, C. E. (2023). Social emotional learning in schools: The importance of educator competence. *Journal of Research on Leadership Education, 18*(1), 3–39. https://doi.org/10.1177/19427751211014920

Goldberg, J. (2016, July 30). *It takes a village to determine the origins of an African proverb*. NPR. https://www.npr.org/sections/goatsandsoda/2016/07/30/487925796/it-takes-a-village-to-determine-the-origins-of-an-african-proverb

Greene, P. (2022, August 11). There is no teacher shortage. So why is everyone talking about it? *Forbes*. https://www.forbes.com/sites/petergreene/2022/08/09/there-is-no-teacher-shortage-so-why-is-everyone-talking-about-it/

Gunn, T. M., & McRae, P. A. (2021). Better understanding the professional and personal factors that influence beginning teacher retention in one Canadian province. *International Journal of Educational Research Open, 2*, Article 100073. https://doi.org/10.1016/j.ijedro.2021.100073

Gunn, T. M., & McRae, P. A. (2024, November 11–13). A longitudinal trend analysis of early career teachers: Five years of data collection and analysis examining professional and personal factors affecting retention in one Canadian province. In *Proceedings of the 17th annual International Conference of Education, Research and Innovation* (pp. 5573–5579). https://doi.org/10.21125/iceri.2024.1355

Hattie, J. A., & Donoghue, G. M. (2016). Learning strategies: A synthesis and conceptual model. *Science of Learning, 1*(1), 1–13.

Hawking, S. (2018). *Brief answers to the big questions*. Random House Large Print.

Hobson, A. J. (2002). Student teachers' perceptions of school-based mentoring in initial teacher training (ITT). *Mentoring & Tutoring: Partnership in Learning, 10*(1), 5–20. https://doi.org/10.1080/13611260220133117

Homer. (2003). *The odyssey* (R. Fagles, Trans.). Penguin Classics. (Original work published ca. 8th century BCE)

Hunzicker, J. (2017). From teacher to teacher leader: A conceptual model. *International Journal of Teacher Leadership, 8*(2), 1–27.

Ingersoll, R. M., & Kralik, J. M. (2004, February). The impact of mentoring on teacher retention: What the research says. *Research Review: Teaching Quality*. Education Commission of the States. https://www.gse.upenn.edu/pdf/rmi/ECS-RMI-2004.pdf

Ingersoll, R. M., & Strong, M. (2011). The impact of induction and mentoring programs for beginning teachers: A critical review of the research. *Review of Educational Research, 81*(2), 201–233. https://doi.org/10.3102/0034654311403323

Johnson, W. B. (2019). *The power of informal mentoring: Creating a mentoring network that works*. Routledge.

Jotkoff, E. (2022, February 1). *NEA survey: Massive staff shortages in schools leading to educator burnout; alarming number of educators indicating they plan to leave the profession* [Press release]. National Education Association. https://www.nea.org/about-nea/media-center/press-releases/nea-survey-massive-staff-shortages-schools-leading-educator-burnout-alarming-number-educators

Keller-Schneider, M., Zhong, H. F., & Yeung, A. S. (2020). Competence and challenge in professional development: Teacher perceptions at different stages of career. *Journal of Education for Teaching, 46*(1), 36–54.

Knight, J. (2019). Instructional coaching for implementing visible learning: A model for translating research into practice. *Education Sciences, 9*(2), 101.

Kraft, A., Blazar, D., & Hogan, D. (2018). The effect of teacher coaching on instruction and achievement: A meta-analysis of the causal evidence. *Review of Educational Research, 88*(4). https://doi.org/10.3102/0034654318759268

Long, A., Hagermoser Sanetti, L., Collier-Meek, M., Gallucci, J., Altschaefl, M., & Kratochwill, T. (2016). An exploratory investigation of teachers' intervention planning and perceived implementation barriers. *Journal of School Psychology*, *55*, 1–26. https://doi.org/10.1016/j.jsp.2015.12.002

Marley, B. (1977). Three little birds [Song]. On *Legend*. Island Records.

Maxwell, J. C. (2015). *The leadership handbook: 26 critical lessons every leader needs*. Thomas Nelson.

McGivern, A. (Host). (2025, January 7). Oprah Winfrey—A mentor is someone who allows you to see the hope inside yourself (No. 373) [Audio podcast episode]. *In The Daily Quote*. https://greatnewspodcast.com/captivate-podcast/oprah-winfrey-a-mentor-is-someone-who-allows-you-to-see-the-hope-inside-yourself/

Mentoring Complete. (2014, January 27). *Help us to celebrate mentors during National Mentoring Month*. https://www.mentoringcomplete.com/help-us-to-celebrate-mentors-during-national-mentoring-month/

Mötley Crüe. (1989). Kickstart my heart [Song]. On *Dr. feelgood*. Elektra Records.

Ogange, B. (2023, October 12). *Reflections on World Teachers' Day 2023: Can we reverse the global teacher shortage?* Commonwealth of Learning. https://www.col.org/news/reflections-on-world-teachers-day-2023-can-we-reverse-the-global-teacher-shortage/

Ontario College of Teachers. (2020). Annual report: Setting the standard for great teaching. https://reports.oct.ca/2020

Oxford University Press. (2025). Maintenance. In *Oxford English Dictionary*. https://www.oed.com/dictionary/maintenance_n?tab=factsheet#38649336

Peck, M. S. (1998). *The different drum: Community making and peace* (2nd Touchstone ed.). Simon and Schuster.

Pirsig, R. M. (1975). *Zen and the art of motorcycle maintenance*. Bantam.

quoteresearch. (2014, April 6). *Quote origin: They may forget what you said, but they will never forget how you made them feel*. Quote Investigator. https://quoteinvestigator.com/2014/04/06/they-feel/

Reddy, L. A., Lekwa, A., & Shernoff, E. (2021). Comparison of the effects of coaching for general and special education teachers in high-poverty urban elementary schools. *Journal of Learning Disabilities*, *54*(1), 36–53.

Robinson, K., & Aronica, L. (2015). *Creative schools: The grassroots revolution that's transforming education*. Penguin.

Rodgers, K., Vescio, V., Burns, J., & Gibbs, L. (2018). The role of preservice teacher coaching in clinically rich teacher education. In D. Hoppey & D. Yendol-Hoppey (Eds.), *Outcomes of high-quality clinical practice in teacher education* (pp. 66–84). Information Age.

Saunders, A. F., Wakeman, S., Cerrato, B., & Johnson, H. (2024). Professional development with ongoing coaching: A model for improving educators' implementation of evidence-based practices. *Teaching Exceptional Children*, *56*(6), 430–439.

Schön, D. A. (2017). *The reflective practitioner: How professionals think in action*. Routledge.

Shank, M. K., & Santiague, L. (2021). Classroom management needs of novice teachers. *The Clearing House: A Journal of Educational Strategies, Issues and Ideas*, *95*(1), 26–34. https://doi-org.proxy1.lib.uwo.ca/10.1080/00098655.2021.2010636

Sherin, M., Jacobs, V., & Philipp, R. (Eds.). (2011). *Mathematics teacher noticing*. Routledge. https://doi.org/10.4324/9780203832714

TED. (2015, September 15). *Bring on the learning revolution! Ken Robinson* [Video]. YouTube. https://www.youtube.com/watch?v=kFMZrEABdw4&ab_channel=TED

Think Baby Names. (2023). *Mentor*. https://www.thinkbabynames.com/meaning/1/Mentor

UNESCO. (2022). *Transforming education from within: Current trends in the status and development of teachers; World Teachers' Day 2022*. https://unesdoc.unesco.org/ark:/48223/pf0000383002

Van Bergen, P., McGrath, K., & Quin, D. (2020). Nurturing close student–teacher relationships. In L. J. Graham (Ed.), *Inclusive education for the 21st century* (1st ed., pp. 296–316). Routledge. https://doi.org/10.4324/9781003116073-16

van der Linden, S., van der Meij, J., & McKenney, S. (2022). Teacher video coaching, from design features to student impacts: A systematic literature review. *Review of Educational Research, 92*(1), 114–165.

van Es, E. A., Stockero, S. L., Sherin, M. G., Van Zoest, L. R., & Dyer, E. (2015). Making the most of teacher self-captured video. *Mathematics Teacher Educator, 4*(1), 6–19. https://doi.org/10.5951/mathteaceduc.4.1.0006

Walker, T. (2021, November 12). Getting serious about teacher burnout. *NEA Today*. https://www.nea.org/nea-today/all-news-articles/getting-serious-about-teacher-burnout

Walker, T. (2022a, February 1). *Survey: Alarming number of educators may soon leave the profession*. National Education Association. https://www.nea.org/advocatingfor-change/new-from-nea/survey-alarming-number-educators-may-soon-leaveprofession

Walker, T. (2022b, April 14). *Beyond burnout: What must be done to tackle the educator shortage*. National Education Association. https://www.nea.org/advocating-forchange/new-from-nea/beyond-burnout-what-must-be-done-tackle-educatorshortage

Will, M. (2023, December 15). The teaching profession in 2023 (in charts). *Education Week*. https://www.edweek.org/teaching-learning/the-teaching-profession-in-2023-in-charts/2023/12

Index

CORWIN

To help every educator help every student

We believe	that every single student deserves a great education
We believe	that knowing our impact is both a privilege and a responsibility
We believe	that a fair, stable, and thriving society is built on education

Zeitfracht Medien GmbH
Ferdinand-Jühlke-Straße 7
99095 Erfurt, Deutschland
produktsicherheit@kolibri360.de